The Philatelist

by

Tito Perdue

Books by Tito Perdue

Lee (1991)
The New Austerities (1994)
Opportunities in Alabama Agriculture (1994)
The Sweet-Scented Manuscript (2004)
Fields of Asphodel (2007)
The Node (2011)
Morning Crafts (2013)
Reuben (2014)
The Builder: William's House I (2016)
The Churl: William's House II (2016)
The Engineer: William's House III (2016)
The Bachelor: William's House IV (2016)
Cynosura (2017)
Philip (2017)
Though We Be Dead, Yet Our Day Will Come (2018)
The Bent Pyramid (2018)

The Philatelist

by

Tito Perdue

Standard American Publishing Company-
Brent, Alabama
2020

CONTENTS

One

Besot with cruelty, time persists at a steady pace. Myself, I had retreated into my neglected garden and by the end of May had sown a full one-eighth acre in pulse beans, parsnips, collards, and potatoes. I will go so far as also to admit that in order to discourage visitors I had taken unto myself a starving dog who had weighed more than seventy pounds, even in his dilapidated state. But here I bring to a stop any further discussion of myself, my life and times, and of how I had come to occupy this special moment in the country's dwindling history.

Two

My house is a good house, and the dog loves it, too. From across the street it might seem a shabby place, for which reason he and I no longer indulged that point of view. But as to the *interior* of our rather unordinary dwelling, the rooms are tall but narrow, so tall indeed that only by means of a high-wattage bulb assisted by a flashlight could a person finally descry the ceiling overhead. Many years ago, a yellow moth had settled there and perished, remaining a landmark as it were, hardly visible through the accumulation of cigarette smoke.

As for the rest, my home has fourteen rooms on several levels, trapezoidal spaces, some of them, congested with books and other cultural materials requisite for a person of my type. I also own good reserves of canned foods, dehydrated milk, purified water, smoked hams, and some hundred-weight of dog bones for the animal who hasn't yet vouchsafed to me his quondam name. I do believe we could hold out in this place, we twain, for months, or until great balls of fire (forecast by me) at last come rolling down from the encompassing hills.

We have our own peas and beans, too (see above), and books and stamps enough to satisfy our joint requirements

I won't mention at this time the condition of the upstairs rooms, the attic, the cellar, nor especially the parlor, an incongruity left over from the Victorian period. Nor do I speak of my neighbors; of them I most particularly do not wish to speak at this time.

They live on the corner in a blue frame house that reiterates some of the more attractive features of my own hundred-year-old house. A modern family incorporating several highly unlike sexualities, the father has lately been retrogendered into a pretty good facsimile of his original self, and can even sometimes be seen shoveling snow in a more or less manly fashion. The mother, on the other hand, the bohemian of the family, is now being given important roles in the kabuki theatre on Second Avenue. Meanwhile her son, an esteemed surgeon specializing in heart cockles, is employed by Massapequa Hospital as a part-time instructor in transactional levitation. He has three children of his own, products of liaisons with a black woman recently let out on probation, and a Navaho priestess from somewhere in the Southwest. His wife, the official one, has contributed three further children to the household, as also a fourth individual fetched here from a clinic in Romania. A victim of cocaine and type II carbohydrates, the youngest of the daughters is said to be living with a Taoist futures trader and yoga instructor out on Staten Island. Taken as a whole, the group has two, possibly three grandmothers forming a "tag team," so to speak, of transgressive-looking personalities coming and going at all hours.

I will admit that I did make one effort to befriend these people, which is to say until they began to befriend me back. A week or two of this, and we seemed to have silently consented to have nothing further to do with each other.

I have a neighbor on the other side as well, a retired professor of some sort who lives alone in a house larger even than my own. A disturbed individual, he appears to enjoy his life in New York City.

But I'm by no means certain that I'll continue with this little diary, if that's what it proves to be, and whether I should allow myself to nostalgicize over an earlier period that really wasn't anywhere near as good as we know damn well it was. But I've digressed.

Three

No one was happier than me, which is to say until I began to dip into the prose confabulations of that iniquitous *Leward Pefley*, whom I hold at fault for a number of other things as well. However, to be fair in all things, it wasn't he who inflicted life upon me at this most ill-chosen time in history. Of course you must realize that in those days to bring children into the world wasn't the same transgression and moral crime that it has since become. A man in 1950—and I don't ask you to believe this—could support a numerous family out of his own sole efforts alone, and never need send his roommate and/or her offspring out to earn additional incomes. Nor made to suffer that onerous surcharge for having partnered within his own race.

To speak of friends and colleagues requires me to mention those friends and colleagues, a heterogeneous group comprising neither real friends nor genuine colleagues, nor very much of anything else. Daily do I shave and dress, force myself into a pair of pretty good shoes, and then impel myself down to the intersection of Martin Luther King, Jr. and 33rd Street, where for the past two years my car pool partners have gathered me up and carried me off to a thirty-story office building made chiefly of glass. Riding in silence while at the same time examining the back of the heads of the three men sitting just in front of me—engineer, bureaucrat, regulator—I felt obliged to speak:

"Dreadful weather."

All three men turned to look at one another.

"Hey, we got us a *meteorologist* for Christ's sakes!" Lester said. The single worst human being of the whole postmodern era, he played golf on weekends and used an after-shave lotion. I blushed, at the same time producing a smile so weak and artificial that I blushed again on behalf of that as well, an "epiphenomenal" reaction, to use the sort of language these people abhor. Truth was, this Lester was a pale and thin sort of entity, and even had I one hand tied behind my back, I could easily have snapped his neck in half. I could see clearly where two of his frail vertebrae (one frailer than the other) ran down into his collar.

"Epi what?"

"Phenomenal. Epiphenomenal."

"Damn, Hugh! Where do you get that stuff?"

I opted to remain silent for the following time. We were passing through a Dominican neighborhood, recently pacified, where an alert person like me in a speedy car like ours could catch glimpses of the contents and personnel of many of the little stores and shops. I spied a fat woman with a stereotypical face, and behind her a half-opened door wherein someone lay sleeping. Came next the vision of some fifteen evil-looking and self-despising men squandering their benefits at a neon-illuminated bar that ran back into the depths of the building. Myself, I've always preferred blue and purple for neon signs, but couldn't really complain about the virid green that mixed and matched so well with the quality of the tavern's clientele.

I earnestly did not wish to report to work that day, not with the weather the way it was and more threatening. Turning my attention to home, I was confident that the dog had preempted my favorite place already, which is to say that ancient rocking chair with the gingham cushion and broken slat. A person of my disposition can find perfect happiness watching the rain from a perch such as that, provided only he had his stamp album in his lap and a cup of coffee near at hand. Provided of course that he had thunder and lightning, too, and the sight of little birds sheltering concernedly anent the late-autumn leaves of my walnut tree. That was when I recognized that the driver had been, and still was speaking to me.

"Absolutely!" I answered, which seemed to satisfy them. By this time we were moving through a black precinct where I caught sight of a recumbent garbage can in which could be seen two hundred coffee grinds, a saturated menstrual pad, and a gallon jug holding the residue of what looked either like wine or something worse.

Me, I was hardened to it. All men, after all, are created equal, a truism vouchsafed us by that most ignominious of the founders. Not to forget the women, equal too, one of them now pressing languidly down the sidewalk in her bathrobe. And after I had spent so many years trying not to be intolerant about such matters! Saw I then a dog, devoured by mange, dragging his chain behind him. (Now if only I could divest myself of all standards, I might still be the most tolerant of persons.)

The Whimple Street unemployment office now came into view on the right-hand side, a doleful sight spilling over with the living discards who had proved digitally inept. "Can you retrofogame the lateral i/v/o sylogrades?" Without a doubt, the country needs more immigrants.

By 8:41 the office building, the same in which I had wasted seventeen years, shunted into view. The construction workers of New York have built hundreds of fine, tall, and aspirational buildings, but only then to stand by and watch them fill with businesspersons. I experienced a sharp pain in my kidney, a Monday morning symptom that intensified as we drew to within a few hundred yards of the place. I couldn't yet identify the silhouettes in the fifth-floor window, though clearly they were those of human beings. A woman was taking off her coat, doing it in the brisk way that showed how glad she was the weekend was over and she was back at work. Having then settled at her desk, she began working on her nails. I felt a headache coming on. Devoid of value, her activities enabled her to forget that time was rushing by, that she was inscribed on death's agenda, and that the world contained innumerable books and postage stamps that neither of us at end of day had time enough to analyze. These were the reasons I was near to tears when finally our two-tone digitized Dacia came to a halt in the parking lot.

"S'matter, Hugh?"

"Monday!" I replied.

I arrived at my desk nine minutes too early, but atoned for it by fidgeting with my tie while at the same time opening and shutting the drawer that held the remains of a bottle of aspirin, an anthology of eighteenth-century English pastoral verse, and a just-released two-volume biography of an out-of-favor Hungarian philosopher. Not that ever I had been given time by my employer—I do not exactly know who my employer really is—given time to read more than ten pages of the introduction to the first volume and none at all in the second. (My employer, to revert to that, is a semi-governmental organization assigned to the collection of information related to a whole raft of things.) Codenamed "Goofy." I was assigned mostly to abstracting, indexing, and critiquing industrial and agricultural reports emanating mainly from East Europe. What, they feared another Marxo-Fascist upsurge, those who paid my wages?

"Can't be too careful," I frequently said.

I had my morning éclair and coffee while at the same time scanning the city's most prominent and most loathsome newspaper. We were not of course allowed to utilize tobacco products, nor maintain firearms and ammunition in any part of our clothing or desks, nor the cloakroom neither. I did have an 8 x 10 photo of the young Corneliu Codreanu in a stand-up frame, confident that none of these people could identify the hero. "My cousin," I lied. "Served in the Police Action in Honduras." Other photographs adorned my cubicle.

Today's newspaper: A black girl had been offended

in Idaho, and a team of psychiatrists were on the way. A group of well-meaning immigrants had capsized in a mid-Atlantic squall. Racism was suspected. Following the accession of Kirgizstan, the European Union had captured an estimated twenty percent of the Central Asian market. Page three showed an angry crowd of white liberals demanding their voting rights be cancelled. Though locked in two patent disputes, a software company had devised a capability that required a change in the Bill of Rights. On the bright side, a lesbian movie star had been named ambassador to France. Bismuth futures were up, the trade balance down, and experts were recommending a variety of strategies.

Four

I never wanted to continue with this "log" of mine, or anyway not until when for reasons to be explained later, I've decided to pick up where I left off two days ago. My approach requires me to justify myself, to give gifts, to offer flattery to everyone, and never ever to cheat on taxes. And isn't every member of an alien species wise to do the same? Dare I ignore sporting events? To openly expose my politics? Was I to confess my preference for some human races (one actually) over others? Was I, in short, to let myself be transported by majority vote direct to the guillotine? Was I, etc., etc., and so forth? Lead the nation to the sunlit uplands of human inequality? Hell, no. And do it all by myself alone?

It was too much, and anyway I adore my role as an undercover agent. I can think my baleful thoughts, thoughts that would astound the world and leave the population gasping. I might turn my back on sporting events and carry with me (either in a satchel or balanced on top my head) the most pernicious of my books and music, and the other accoutrements that cause ordinary people to confront their own mediocrity, and mayhap yours as well.

Having dealt with the éclair and coffee, I settled into my niche. It was 9:04 by the clock when at last I turned on my rebuilt computer and waited for the picture of myself at age 24, the most iconic of my icons, to resolve itself on the screen. It was an heirloom, that machine, and one that had endured a great many repairs and, yes, a lot of unfair ridicule. Someone had sent an email, but I was smart enough to erase it. Even here, here among my fellow salarypersons, I had enemies, bad people, feminists mostly, impervious to my courtesies and graceful behavior. Came then the news via that same computer, a recitation of generic misfortunes beginning with the disquieting decline in the price of sorghum futures.

There was a woman—call her Tiffany—who sat just fifteen feet to my right-hand side. I had been expecting her to speak, she who was generally so full of cheery greetings; instead, today, she appeared to have been discouraged by the sorghum business.

"G'morning!" said I, aiming for the hole in her left ear. "I like that scarf!" (An unexceptional article carrying images of daffodils. It might have sufficed for a dusting cloth, nothing else.) "It matches your eyes!" (The eye on the far side of her nose, that was possible. It most certainly did *not* match the nearer one that had required New York's most implausible prosthetic. Apparently she had been hit by a dart at some age, and the color of her iris had largely drained away.)

"Just lovely."

"Oh, you're just so *gallant*, Hugh. But keep it up!"

I smiled, holding it for about as long as I could. She was the mother of two daughters by half a dozen men, and so imbrued in post-modern philosophy that she couldn't understand why things hadn't worked out as well as they should.

There were of course other Tiffanies in that room, most of them divorced or unmarriageable or addicted to psychotropic drugs. I do not mention the person nearest the door, who might be a woman, too. Could anything be more dispiriting for a person of my kind than having to go on day after day, pretending to be no better than one's associates? Meantime my computer, "Tiffany" I call it, was throwing up all sorts of material that had no bearing whatsoever on my assignment, insofar as I understood said assignment. In brief, I was being asked to find corroborating evidence of the agricultural situation in Nepal, and because I knew nothing of the preposterous language of that place, I was to pass the whole mess through a translation service maintained either by the Army or by a certain fiber purchasing conglomerate under the direction of MLK University. For me the work was rote, and yet it was for this that I'd been bonded, insured, fingerprinted, and interrogated annually over the whole of my career. More vitally, my pass bore a color photograph in profile, a list of felonies, and a DNA hologram that described my chemistry and supposed propensities.

I continued apace, laboring away the hours. On Saturday last I had visited the opera, and still wasn't able to free my head of the insidious female duet in *Norma*. Good music, and like all music of that degree, it was like to drive me insane. Just then I was interrupted by the bozo, a one-time soccer player who occupied the diagonal cubicle. He was a large person, and his trousers were so much too short that anyone could see the scars on his right front leg that very frequently extruded into what ought have been my own private area.

"Hey, Hugh!" (His voice was loud enough, bringing several workers out of their concentration.)

"Still here." (My voice, too, was loud enough, and after traveling the length of the very narrow and tapering room, impinged on the portrait of the company President and bounced right back again.)

"You watch the game? The Peacocks?"

"You bet! Those ole Peacocks. Really something, waddn't it?"

He was not a bad person, Bozo, and would have been even better had he been weaned instead on the female of his parents. Today he had done a poor job of shaving and had a tad of toilet paper adhering to his chin. It was a mystery to all of us how he had qualified for this job, though it might probably be related to our Deputy Chief, a man never glimpsed by any of us, but a well-known soccer fan all the same. Accordingly it was incumbent on me to listen to his (Bozo's, not the supervisor's) patter. Meanwhile I was beginning to tap into some hitherto-unpublished numbers concerning cashew imports/exports taking place between two of our country's most reliable dependencies.

I had not meant to suggest that we two males, Bozo and I, had been forced into service amidst a gaggle of post-normal women, even if to say so would have been accurate. Some of these were pretty and some were not, and one was an Ashkenazi woman who before his suicide had insisted that her son become a doctor and a lawyer at the same time. In truth she re-

ally was a good-looking woman with a definite philatelic quality in her profile. It has been said that Hel-
en's breasts were so lovely, the Greeks used the dual
number when referring to her.

These then were the human resources (once called
"people") who occupied our long (thirty-eight feet)
and narrow (nineteen feet) cell. From my position
near the front, it looked approximately like a seven
hundred-square foot working space for twenty to
twenty-five persons, a total that fluctuated with the
weather and manifest attendance of the personnel.

Five

I have chosen to retire! Or anyway just as soon as I
have earned my pension. It is true that I could take
retirement somewhat earlier than that, but only at the
cost of about two hundred and fifty Euros per month.
Two-fifty, an amount sufficient for half a dozen out-
of-print books with original covers on them. Or, ex-
pressed differently, eight opera tickets. Or a certain
nineteenth-century Chinese postage stamp for my
collection. A double handful of Kellogg Pep cereal
pin-backs, and funds enough left over for a second-
hand .45-caliber revolver available from my personal
pawnbroker. Or, more imperative still, an improved
dietary for my dog. Indeed, I needed that money and
was determined to have it, even if I must go back to
digging for truffles in Central Park.

It was with these thoughts in mind that I took a
day's sick leave, and after harvesting my first full
night's sleep since my last illness, opened up the foot-
locker at the foot of my cot and drew out the third
volume of my Islamic collection, following which I

micturated in the place reserved for that and washed my face.

Next, I put on Walton's *Violin Concerto* and then opened to Persia in my superbly illustrated stamp album printed many years ago in pre-independent Latvia. The dog had been fed and was content and knew not to annoy me at times like this. True, it *was* somewhat windy out-of-doors, and from time to time I could hear one or another of the shutters slamming against the sheetrock. Or pick up the sound of an automobile passing in the street. And yet I remained calm throughout the morning. I had locked the gate and had parked a sawhorse across the walk leading to my front door.

Very good. And so at 10:27 exactly I opened the album and turned to page 614. It's true that I have a very decent collection of Persia, even perhaps among the best in the city, judging by its reputation. Acting with caution, I turned one entire page at the same time and laid it flat, a noiseless tactic that revealed of a sudden a swatch of colorful "values," as we call them, showing the same ruthless Shah in a twelve-unit series. There's enough history on that page to fill an encyclopedia, even apart from Thistlewaite's wonderful monograph on early Iranian postmarks. Certifiably the most polyhistorical of all persons—he was also a cello virtuoso—that man's cognizance seemed to reach all the way back to the Cenozoic and the philatelic history of those awful times.

I owned precisely ten of those twelve stamps, a personal failure that left two loathsome blank spaces on the page. At one time I had pasted two defective issues here, but I need to make it clear at the outset that imperfection is not in my nature, neither when at home, or sleeping, or at my station when at work. I had rather amputate my own foot than to accept even the most innocuous faults of society, of life, and of ordinary people especially. Ordinary people? Am I then so great that I can talk like that? No, absolutely not. Save on Wednesdays of course, and the occasional Saturday perhaps.

Six

Wednesday having arrived, I leapt up in joyful alacrity and headed off to work. The day was bright and sunny, but instead of bookstores and stamp and coin traders, I found only jewelry stores and women's shops along my route. Judging by what was visible, a stranger would assume the town had six times as many women as the other kind. Rotten with wealth, this macabre city was like an overripe fruit full of putrescence and prone at any moment to explode. I had awoken in unusually good spirits, and although the Sun today was white as platinum and giving off a humming sound, I quickly relapsed into my authentic self. I heard voices (shards of broken glass they seemed) emitted by policemen, bus drivers, and delivery people. I perceived a woman marching at my side and immediately began to walk more quickly lest it appear that we comprised a partnership of some kind. Her hair was pink as cotton candy, while her mouth was like a suction cup. Her teeth were good, pretty good, and never mind that one had died and was out-of-parallel with the others. Her chin came to a point, as eventually it must. But of course the main things were her eyes, furious-looking instruments half-hidden under granulated lids.

We had come into a realm of glass buildings where

even a mediocre soprano could have brought the whole mess down about our ears. I slowed, hoping the woman—we both wanted to be free of each other—would move ahead of me. Her heels, longer than pencils, punched holes in the cement and made noises like a teletype machine. We moved past one of the few places in Manhattan where Christians were wont to gather, in this case a congregation of snake handlers with an ambulance standing by. We passed a department store, the window full of manikins in erotic underwear. Saying nothing, we continued hastily past the memorial display of Monica and Bill in the buccal position. Remove these evanescent shops from Manhattan and the economy takes the bookstores down with them. The woman had also slowed, embarrassing the both of us. Finally I turned to her, saying in my jocular fashion:

"Shall we honeymoon in Hawaii?"

She never smiled.

"I feel that two children ought be enough, yes?"

I have said that the demise of women's shops would imperil the nation. But that was before I went down into a hole in the ground where right away I detected two desiderata of that gender waiting for the subway in heels and hose, earrings, skirts, hairdos, perfume, and ankle bracelets. A cynic might say they wanted to draw attention to themselves.

They wanted to draw attention to themselves.

Years ago, I had laid claim to a certain seat on the morning subway, and since that time I've often wondered whatever happened to the X-ray technician, the insurance man, and the shoe salesman who previously had shared with me that car. I have the highest esteem for such people, for those who have taken on the most boring activities that modernity has invented in order to enhance the lives of the fortunate and the rich. Today I found myself squeezed in between two well-dressed men exchanging pages of the same newspaper back and forth. I was not too dignified to steal glimpses of the headlines, fore and aft:

A famous actress had allowed her left nipple to be seen.

The bombing campaign in Bolivia was continuing apace. An American airman had been shot down and was missing, while in retaliation some four hundred farmers and other terrorists had been slain.

Copper futures, down at 6:00 PM last night had recovered by 9:22.

Interracial marriage numbers were improving in the South, and Congress had withdrawn part of the National Guard.

Further information was not visible to me, whereupon my attention turned to the cleaning woman, as I assumed her to be, sitting just opposite me beneath a specious advertisement for erectile devices. She was tired, overweight, and in her exhaustion she had let her knees fall apart, an unpleasant scene. But how would I like it, to dust the furniture and mop the floor in order to make a bunch of goddamn businesspersons happy? And had I not always done my own furniture and floors, howeverso seldom it might have been? And how was it that our system punished this good woman on behalf of the scum sitting at my side?

I was dreaming about blood and revolution, anthrax spores and the burning of New York, when just that moment the train came to the right place and I must perforce abandon my seat to the bozo who had been hovering over me for the past minutes. You should have seen how the world's most prosperous, luckiest, and most essential people leapt from the train to go racing in a panic for their office buildings. A dignified individual in a grey suit smote me by accident with his briefcase and continued running forward. In 480 BC, the Athenians had rallied to defend their city. But this?

Consumables were faring well, but by the time I reached my own building, rutabaga options had fallen once again. Forcing my way through the bozos mustering in the hall, I espied an apprentice adult, as I calls 'em, a young one wearing a fractal tie. Destined for greatness, the boy had not only accepted every meme in circulation, but also those that hadn't been invented yet. I envied him of course (how could I not?), him and all other people blessed with the gift for believing what they should.

There was a little chocolate cupcake waiting on my desk. Was I the most popular member of our group, or not? I smiled, twice, complimented Tiffany on her new blouse and then, fueled by coffee and chocolate icing, set to work with the sort of energy that might endure for up to fifteen minutes. Seen from the other stations, my double-breasted suit was cerulean blue and my facial expression entirely neutral. My hair, the best part of me, looked as if I had tried very hard to comb it but had failed. They like that, women do, sincerity mixed with failure.

Will night *never* come? I had been on duty for the better part of half an hour, but still had nine full hours before crepuscule. Darkness comes early in the Adirondacks and other good places, but even there the unspeakable sun was currently at work exposing all the ugliness of the visible world. Wise people stay in bed, waiting for the night. One sole distraction, namely that one of the Tiffanies, a comely girl, was dressed in a skirt a good ten inches shorter than the law ought have allowed. They do it on purpose, women and girls. However—and you have already divined this in me—I have inured myself against these ploys. My second wife had also been alluring in her clothes, if rather less so at other times. And besides, I'm a full 52 years old.

Today I had been assigned to monitor a country that I'm not allowed to name, a square-shaped territory in the extreme southwest of the European continent. Concerning the Spanish language, I know enough of that not to need the translation service. Clearly this NATO ally of ours was beginning to chafe under the demands of the world's premier economic and military power. Must she indeed participate in the bombing of Bolivia?

"Let Spain be Spain!" I wanted to say, concerning the unnamed country alluded to just an inch or two above. I oughtn't even write that down on paper, save that no one shall ever see it.

Came two o'clock I began to feel a headache coming on. There was no need for me to seek permission, not after so many years of service, and I was able to exit the building while attracting the notice only of the bozo who operated the information desk, a "friend" of mine, as I had permitted him to imagine. We smiled, each to each. The day was sweet, mellow, and melancholy, and reminded me of a certain Hungarian stamp. Yes, there *were* a number of bookshops and antiquaries here, one conscientious publisher (since closed down), and some five or six million digestive tracts that fomented daily enough waste material to fertilize the Asian steppes. I have seen these systems hurrying off to work, going to places they detested in order to perform actions they deplored under supervisors they despised. I wanted to tell them how at one time we used to work at home or on the farm, laboring amongst whom we loved while practicing self-sufficiency, or near it. And hadn't I rather be a wheelwright, or goldsmith, an enamellist, a sixteenth-century printer, or grow seedless avocados on a spread somewhere in the Yucatan?

I proceeded northward along the wide sidewalk that carried to another sandwich-shaped structure also formed primarily of glass. In Aachen, they say, Charlemagne abided happily in a palace made of wood. I was so tired of it, of glass and steel, glossy automobiles, of people's faces inset with gills and glands, of breathing holes and glistening eyes that shift one way and another under random compulsions emanating from the dark side of the cortex. Horrible, and yet this is how for fifty years and more I've looked upon the teeming world. Just then I set eyes upon a small brown immigrant he must have been, his face as vicious as a snake's.

At three o'clock, or just slightly after, I bumbled into a stretch of yellow tape that marked the boundary of the "no go" region where the police and census-takers refuse to go. Although very bad for the country, the presence of these people was said to be good for the economy. Here heroin was in popular use, and homicides were reported in round numbers. I admit it, that I harbor some respect, just some, for people who turn away from normative careers, from advertising and public relations, from the law and social work, from mainstream publishing and every other form of exertion that engrosses numbers of unrelated persons. It is true of course that the really interesting subjects would bore most such people quite to death.

I went on. It's my intention to know this city, to face up to it bravely inasmuch as I consider it a large-scale mock-up of the human soul itself in decadent phase. There's a place downtown where for a high fee, one can watch derelicts fight to the death with knives. Under my microscope I once saw a bloated amoeba marshalling a crowd of cowed paramecia. A town, this, where some have no homes and others have fifty-story buildings all their own, and where the inverse ratio between human quality and monetary success moves closer every day to absolute perfection. But mostly my concern is for those who gave their lives for this country, never dreaming it could turn to this.

A crowd had gathered outside the 66th Street Retrogendering Center, where a dispute seemed to be in progress. Crossing hurriedly to attend to it, I almost collided into a large bearded man or woman who offered me a pamphlet of some sort with a photograph on the cover of copulating movie stars. I watched a black woman shuffling toward a chauffeured car, her face a masque of ignorance and putrefaction.

I strolled past a tall, crystalline building whence the country's decision-makers were wont to issue IPOs, leveraged takeovers, etc., etc., and all those other ingenious "instruments" that granted them control equally of racehorses, foreign policy, and seventy-two-hole golf courses. Where were my horses? I have read far more books than any of these. For years now, I have been craving for a merciless dictatorship consecrated to the humiliation of the rich and ignorant. There, in that longed-for place, the women will be as loyal as Penelope, beautiful as Helen, noble as Héloise, and the town crowded with philosophers in lieu of what we see around us.

I had taken three cups of coffee at noon, but now

when it came time to expel them, there wasn't a facility anywhere. Did Lawrence have this problem on his trek to Akaba? I stepped into a department store, but after roving up and down the aisles I found, not a restroom precisely, but rather a pot to pee in, as people say. Strange world, this. A man can get a blowjob here for silver change, but if he needs to piss, or more, he'll have to run back home again!

When in the course of enjoying New York, it's bad practice to avoid the Museum of Modern Art. Even so, I just didn't have the stomach for it on this autumn day. The pedestrians were already startling enough for me. I saw a queer with purple fingernails, and next a starving dog whose face reflected great wonderment as to how it could have come to this. I hastened to buy a quart of milk, but when I returned the creature had altogether disappeared. Another of my headaches was coming on, this one yet more serious than yesterday's. Fortunately for New York, indeed for city people everywhere, I had brought no firearms with me.

Having never actually used a pot to pee in, I finally came to a facility at the corner of Fifth and Priscilla, and after decanting a volume of urine (with blood in it) along with a quart of milk, delayed there long enough to peruse the graffiti. Only here may one see the *true* sentiments of all those men in expensive suits. It was now exactly four minutes past 3:16, and I had miles to go before I'd have to pee again.

Always prepared for the onset of depression, I drifted half unwillingly into a subsurface pawnshop administered by the sort of person one expects in such places. The fellow had accumulated all manner of obsolete wedding rings, photo albums, and a silver saxophone with an autographed baseball nesting in the bell. I looked for, but could not find, second-hand gall bladders available for transplant. And yet, strangely, the few pieces of artwork to be seen, amateur material rendered by housewives and the like, were so much superior to the cultural signifiers in the Museum of Modern Art that I was tempted to invest in them.

The time had moved to 4:02, and I had chosen a route considerably less traveled by. Another three hours and the bars would open, the whores come out, the neon come on, and the New Yorkers could resume sniffing one another's crotches in this most fervent, most vibrant, most moneyed, did I say vibrant already?, most abject place on Earth. Suddenly, just then there came the sound of an ambulance rushing past outside, a noisy vehicle followed by two police cars and some two score of lawyers, journalists, and spectators. The tallest building in New York was on fire! No, not so. No, I was simply hallucinating once again.

For two decades the city fathers had wanted to seize my ancient house in order to widen a street that really oughtn't have come into existence in the first place. Here, long ago, alligators and swamp birds had enjoyed the right of way. Satisfied to find that my abode had *not* been taken from me during my absence, I opened both locks and went to check on my stamp collection. The dog was aggrieved, wherefore I hastened to take two desiccated waffles from the pantry and charge them to overflowing with bacon grease. In his place, I would have chosen to dine more slowly, enjoying the repast, even allowing the substance to sit on the tongue for a while. But not this creature.

No one had disturbed my collection, neither my enemies nor my neighboring fellow philatelic collaborator identified here simply as "My Fellow Philatelic Collaborator." He knows very well where I keep my albums and has remarked more than once on a certain Honduran airmail that he covets. And no wonder; a copy less perfect than mine has recently changed hands for almost *ten thousand dollars*. Or twenty-three hundred, rather, to be completely candid about it.

The specimen was still there! I examined it under my glass, reminding myself of the least little flaw in the northwest corner that ought not seriously reduce its value on the Manhattan market. To lift the thing and peer more closely at it, I selected my favorite tweezers, a half-ounce implement that acuminates down to spade-like pincers of not much more than a molecule of thickness, atomically speaking. No one could claim the stamp was mint new of course. Judging from the mucilage, it had been used at least once, and had presumably brought the accompanying letter (now lost) to its intended recipient, dwelling God knows where. I would dearly have loved to own that letter and, while never actually reading it, return it to its original consignee.

I again dined on waffles that night, using Vermont syrup and real butter in place of bacon grease, another area in which our tastes diverged, the dog's and mine. While in the kitchen I took the time to roast another two dozen of the things against the future and laid them away in the pantry that also held a robust hoard of liquors and sweets. Someday great balls of fire would come tumbling down Priscilla Street, quarantining the two of us inside. With my radio, my books, my stamps of course, and stocks of food, I looked forward to it.

I rested briefly, on this occasion choosing the up-stairs bed. This might have been a good time to die, if only I were sure the West would go on without me. Instead I fell into a short, exhilarating dream in which the Confederacy had learned to produce nuclear weapons. It was dark when I awoke, and I had to hur-ry if I wanted to be brought up to date by one of the lovely blond women who nowadays gives the news. Today's events had been ambiguous, though it did seem clear that a black person really had been offend-ed rather seriously somewhere in Topeka. Having di-gested that information, I switched over to channel six where the in-house blond was describing the mess in Bolivia. There followed a panel discussion, a lively debate between professors from Harvard and/or Yale. I endured it. Channels nine, ten, eleven, and twelve had been given over respectively to baseball, tennis, bowling, and some of the more memorable football highlights of 1994. We marveled at that transcendent moment when the blue team had stopped the reds on the two-yard line. Finally, at shortly after midnight, I broke open a bottle of brandy with a unicorn on the label and initiated the long and tedious process of get-ting back to sleep again. I prefer to dream of prison breaks, especially when the screws get the worst of it. Other dreams of mine generally take place on trains and submarines.

Seven

As promised, I've explained a great many things al-ready, and as time goes on, I expect to explain even more. Why, for example, have I chosen to continue with this account?

There's a woman who sits down the aisle, a late-middle-age Tiffany who appears to be even older than me. Having done two years' duty on the front lines in Tajikistan, having lost her husband, having learnt the clownish language of that referenced country, and having now to earn a living, she's been sitting here for the past several years mulling silently over her past life and sadness, in view of which no one dares disparage her or complain about her work. Truth is, she's a self-effacing sort of type who takes directions without demur and who seems to understand my standing in the organization as owed to my longitude, or longevity I should have said, in service to national security. I mention as well that she has contributed no small number of rather scarce stamps to my collection, including one in particular. And in short I believe it is largely on account of her, and others like her, that I have gradually over the years learned to appreciate, even to *love* my fellow creatures, most of them doing about as well as their genetic inheritance allows. Not that I intend to wallow in this kind of sentimentality, this bathos, this "television approach" to humanity's collective "excellence," or that any of what I've said has to do with why I've chosen to continue with this report that you hold in your hand.

Once, when I was ten, I saw the remains of a man cut in half from an airplane crash, permitting me to see what stuff humans are. Composed primarily of water and snot, of secretions and emanations, gas, saliva, excrement, enzymes, and everything nasty, it's wonderful how this wise and generous race of people is working overtime to build machines to make themselves unneeded, a barefoot, or as I had intended rather to say, a bootless effort to be sure.

She was toiling conscientiously when I came in, "eavesdropping" on a revolutionary poet in San Salvador, a naïve young man who hadn't the least understanding that his lines even now were flooding into one of the federal databanks lying several hundred feet below ground somewhere in Colorado. I thanked her, Tiffany, for her good work, and then voyaged over to my own station where a warm éclair was waiting, marmalade on it. (I must at all times have sweet things in the morning.) Today the coffee had been prepared to the correct formulation, for which I gave unspoken thanks to the Tiffany in the back row who had proved highly knowledgeable in Serbo-Croatian speech.

My computer was blushing like a 1950s jukebox, and right away I used it to tune in to the New York Stock Exchange. I was committed to the programmed purchase of a certain well-known index fund on Mondays when prices usually fell, and then to selling an analogous fund on Friday, when prices went higher about seven times out of twelve. I am almost ashamed to report the unconscionable profits I earned, or "acquired" rather, to use the right word, in this way. Starting with just $5,000, I had gradually earned a total I can't bring myself to confess. I can say that it brought my retirement about two years closer while at the same time enhancing very importantly my collection of nineteenth-century Japanese issues.

Today, equities were fluctuating within a narrow range. I had speculated disproportionately in Taiwanese shares, believing as I did that these would escalate the moment that country was folded into the mainland. You can imagine the effects of that.

The organization no longer permitted online visitations to gossip sites. Nor were we allowed to buy merchandise, not on "company" time, or involve ourselves in international chess matches, or break into military sites, or inspect the private holdings of celebrities and business leaders. Or ask about our country's gold reserves and how much continued to be there. Shrewd, our administrators, but not so shrewd as to have prohibited us from monitoring stamp auctions taking part continually in the greater American cities.

In the eyes of my supervisor, a simpleton named Bozo, I was doing research. In fact I was looking for the sixpence "Yellow Rhinoceros" issued in the place mistakenly called "Zambia" by modern people. Changing over to the auction in Denver, I was able to access many other African values, but nothing more about "The Rhino," as we collectors call it. Prices are high, and I'd begun to worry that stamp inflation might actually stymie my retirement, set now for February, 2021. Despite all this I *was* able to narrow in on a commemorative issue that portrayed, not rhinoceri indeed, but the world's last surviving ziggurat, a fragile structure brought hither to serve as a gambling palace in Las Vegas. He was a fine engraver, who had chiseled these scenes, and fine, too, the colorist who had made each stamp a slightly variant pastel running through the whole gamut of purples and greens and back again. Magnifying the thing, I imagined at first that I could discern a tiny little muezzin imprecating from the top of that tower, which is to say until I took up my magnifying glass and amended myself.

I run to beauty. It relates to something, does beauty, that exists far more pronouncedly in other realms. And if I've been unfair to my employers in consequence of my aestheticism, yet I've always been able quickly to forgive myself. Next, I called up an exhaustive collection of European classics available at high price, and in the midst of that assortment discerned a variant of my favorite all-time stamp, a melancholy portrayal of old Saint Martin gazing down sadly over the ruined fields of Merovingian France. It's evil of me, I suppose, to compare and contrast this with what's on offer at the Museum of Modern Art.

The West is dying, at which point I withdrew into the men's facility and lit up a cigarette. The spy camera had been out of commission for the last several days, and a person could smoke here in freedom. The graffiti, I'll admit it, was a bit more sophisticated than herebefore, and had been continued over to the ceiling itself. I detected a quotation from Guénon. Meantime my cigarette, fetched here by Somali smugglers in plain envelopes, was good.

Actually the Somalis had come by boat, and not in the plain envelopes that literalistic readers, of which I have far too many, might have imagined. Compiled out of a dark brown weed, those readers might think my cigarette was another of those low-grade products made from ordinary deciduous leaves gathered randomly by the usual extra-legal tobacconists attempting to avoid taxes. Not so. I had looked at the stuff under my microscope back at "headquarters," a slipshod word I use sometimes for "home."

No, my readers are not of course compiled out of a dark brown weed, and I shouldn't have to say it. Normally I take lunch at about 2:30 in the afternoon, hoping in that way to evade anyone who might want to join me. Unfortunately, the bozo had puzzled out my schedule and was waiting. Far the most unintelligent man in the corporation, his eyes were like a rodent's, and his nose had a supernumerary growth on it.

"Join me, if you want to," he said.

(Oh, good!) "Actually," said I, "I have to stop by the

Post Office and . . ."

"No, you don't. Anyway I need a drink."

We strode briskly in the direction of Radeck's Bar and Grill, both of us taking all precaution as not to tread on the high-heeled women who vitiated progress. The sidewalk accommodated twice as many hips as actual women, but as a fancier of both, I didn't mind the walk. I observed a woman in tight pants who was also wearing panties, an aesthetic mistake. And a tall man who had no real chance of ever becoming a real collector, judging by him.

It's good for my reputation sometimes to be seen in company with other employees, wherefore once again I had agreed to expose myself to the conversation of an American. The weather was poor (by my standards), and yet we ventured all the way to a new establishment that by other standards of mine was much too far away and too-well lighted. A much-frequented place, the actual patrons looked as if they'd been designed by a retired scientist with a well-equipped downstairs laboratory. I saw no pair of shoes that could have cost under $200.

We settled at Bozo's favorite table, where our backs were necessarily exposed to anyone in possession of a knife or fork. I knew that we had come to one of the better restaurants when I saw how small the portions were. Myself, I ordered a daiquiri in which the little daiquiris were few and far between, and then followed that up with a white wine that tasted as it should, very like the wine it was. To me, it distinguished itself only by the little shards of cork resting on the bottom of the beaker. Slumbering there, unperturbed by the miniature tides and motions that must surely exist in even so small an ocean as that, the bits of cork reminded me of something I had seen

before in other goblets with other wines and corks. Of
food, I wanted nothing to do with it. The cook was a
fat man in an undershirt. Just then I realized that my
host was and had been speaking for quite some time
now. It was not that he was absolutely ignorant, as I
have perhaps unfairly suggested, but rather that nothing of his had aught to do with any of me and my
somewhat more elevated interests. And besides, the
man was married and full of household concerns: his
wife's complaints, two worthless sons, and crabgrass
problems. He suffered from gastric stones, and in
short his worries were so pedestrian and so predictable that I began to wish for him the sort of experienc-
es that might yet turn him into something more like
me.

We laughed merrily. I never spoke about my work,
save only when among other bozos who believed we
shared the same attitude toward life and things. And,
of course, a few stamp collectors.

By hap, we were positioned near to some undesira-
ble types speaking excitedly of weather reports, gaso-
line mileage, and football scores. I could pick up other
phrases from other regions of the room, but not even
that could force me out of the pleasant smile I had
selected for this occasion. Really, could anything on
Earth be more repellant, more lacking in dignity than
a crowd of mediocrities enjoying each other's presence?

"I've been thinking," I admitted to my tablemate.

"Oh, shit." (He had finished his vegetables and
come at last to the dessert, a complicated assemblage
worth somewhat more than fifteen dollars, to believe
the menu.)

"It's the speed of light, don't you see; we can't visit
other planets because we'd need to go faster than the

speed of light."

"Please, Hugh."

"So all we have to do is load one of these new 'printers,' deceptively so-called, with biologic material instead of ink, and instruct them to print out a human being once they've landed in another galaxy."

"That's real good, Hugh."

"And then that person could 'semaphore' back to us what he's learned!"

"You'd still need to go faster than light, if you want that 'printer' to ever get there. Those stars and whatnot are a far way off, Hugh. *Far.*" (The food had gotten amongst his teeth and he stood in serious need of flossing material.)

"But it would still get there. Eventually."

"Yeah, except we'll both be old men by then."

He was right. The protuberance on his nose had in the meantime touched the gravy, and had picked up a small brown stain about the size of a dot.

"Alright," I persisted, "how about this—we all know that time is an illusion, yes? And that in fact everything that has happened, happened all at once in one fell moment. And so time, so-called, is but a psychological utility that puts experience into order, and allows us to cope with it one item at a time."

"Brilliant, Hugh, just brilliant. Are you *completely* insane?"

Another ten minutes and I could be back at my desk again; instead I used the interval to glance about at my fellow Americans, a pitiable crowd of guilty-looking types resigned to the theory of equality, a murderous code favored especially by bad persons. Neither half-full nor half-empty, those skulls contained on average perhaps a half-gallon of liquid excrement that could be heard sloshing about in there.

It's difficult in circumstances such as these to maintain a placid expression, wherefore I drowned my cigarette in the grinds of my daiquiri, and after leaving a tip, or rather a down payment on one, abandoned the place. There were at least two persons in that postmodern refectory who had looked like Pinkertons to me. I could say more on this topic.

But not just now.

Eight

Today I come to you from this remote city where for the past week I've been watching from my attic window as a thirty-foot (some say thirty-five), thirty-five-foot wall is being put up along the boundary that will divide the Turks from the belligerent Greeks on that side. Built at enormous cost, the legislature sitting in Herkimer had temporarily allowed tobacco products back into use, hoping by that expedient to raise the needed revenue.

I live in the interstices of work and sleep, those few blessed moments between boredom and nightmares when I imagine that I am back at work again. No, wait, I *am* back at work again, as I can verify by the number and the nature of the people on all sides. Just now my attention is fixed upon a bozo in the next aisle, a portly individual rotting from both ends at the same time. He turns and smiles at me, apparently in the belief that we are friends. Caught unprepared, I force myself to reciprocate, which is to say until I let the exercise continue for too long and ended up with an absurd and no doubt unconvincing expression affixed to my face. A sweet human being, generous to all, I was terrified that he, like everyone else in that organization, might offer to have lunch with me, another of the many perils of being a popular person. It was precisely on account of such people that I have begun taking my midday meals in the upstairs toilet, where I'm at liberty to eat my apple, smoke my cigarette, and drink my liquor from a slender flask of aluminum alloy. Which is to say until the custodian spotted my album lying open on the floor. We fought for it, the man surrendering to me at last.

All my life I have wanted to be the only person in the world. Moving from one residence to another, sometimes occupying hotels or mansions, sometimes a library or Thelemite church, I would have time for all the films and stamps and good books that had escaped me in active times. Sleep all day, read all night. With an apartment on the top floor of the tallest building, we could look down, the dog and me, into the burnt remains of a civilization that at one time might almost have been like Greece. That was when the bozo described above as "rotting from both ends" rose and stretched, smiled, and came over to me. We were the best of friends—he believed that.

"Hey chum; how's it going?"

In the afternoon I managed to achieve a great deal less than my salary would have suggested. But at least my colleagues were happy. They each had a position, an income, good shoes, acquaintances, a car, a bed of one's own. What is left to wish for? As happy as ants they were, who come together at night in tight quarters. I wanted to slay the entire bunch of them.

Night did come, albeit about six hours later than desirable. We made the rounds, the dog and me, and after securing the four corners of my forty-three-square-foot backyard, we jumped back inside and locked the door. I could now look forward to as much as full ten hours without human participation, the nearest approach to happiness allowed such people as myself. We ate quickly, relishing the waffles, and in the case of the dog, a bit of left-over sausage that caused his eyes to glow.

I am indebted to my house, and to the bricklayers and carpenters and fresco painters of eighty years ago. In their honor I allowed into my dwelling no piece of furniture younger than me, nor any typewriter that needed electricity, nor any English-language novel written past 1930. Nor was I especially fond of incandescent lamps. Kerosene gives a mellow glow.

Now was the time to take out my collection and magnifying glass and focus on some of the images provided in the classic material prior to 1945. Here one could see castles, battle scenes, portraits both of stern-looking rulers and garden variety human individuals. Those were serious times, those, masculine in character, before the West had lapsed into . . . into that huge black fly who had just then settled on a Hungarian issue that had cost me better than $200 at that time. As bloated as she was on human blood, I dasn't swat the thing lest she do damage to one of the best views of Budapest in my collection.

Turning to Romania, I lingered over the 1941 "fortress and monastery" series of semi-postals showing stone buildings of historical importance, and never mind that the stamps themselves have no antiquarian value. You have already seen, or soon will, that I care only for *aesthetics*, a personality defect that angers some of my philatelic colleagues who actually strive to make money from what ought to be a spiritual project only, beneficial to the soul. Watermarks? Variants?

Mistakes? Perforations? Superior people care nothing for such trivia. Both here and in life itself, art is all. I am even able to enjoy some of the commemoratives of King Carol II, one of Europe's most contemptible men, and the murderer of Codreanu.

A minute of this, I hurried back to Hungary and dawdled over the four values issued under foreign occupation in 1916, a sample of the arrogance that ought to remind us of the gains made by Romania as a result of that conflict. All my life I have wanted to visit those countries to verify they are as awful as commonly believed. I know this, that no country can be all bad that issued the Bulgarian "sunflower" stamps of 1938 (Scott A142).

I haven't mentioned in this context that on Monday I received a tiny glassine envelope holding a full set of early airmails that had cost more than I care to admit. Working slowly with my tweezers, I forced each stamp into the yawning space awaiting them and affixed them permanently to the page, or for at least as long as I am likely to distract myself with this rather ineffective avenue of escape from the postmodern world. Actually, books are better.

And so at two o'clock I leapt to bed, and after dithering with the sheets, my two pillows (one fat one and one thin), my matches and cigarettes, and my worn copy of Kurtagić's large novel, I read efficiently till just past 2:03, whereupon I smothered the lamp and permitted the light to fly from the room and to where it was wanted more.

The night is cold, and the woods full of animals who will freeze tonight. Who but a sadist would have inflicted life upon such creatures, squirrels and birds who know enough about the world not to ask for mercy? There they sit, shuddering in the treetops, wondering what they had done to merit this. The Author of all Suffering I then seemed to see, a bemused man sipping wine in his robe and slippers. For him, the doings back on Earth are but as the affairs of bacilli confined to a thimble in the mansion of time and space.

It was at this point that I fell off into unquiet dreams relating to a number of things.

Nine

My whole purpose has been to give here the reasons for my life and behavior.

Other reasons have to do with events that should have been described earlier, namely my origins, education, opinions, travel, and marriages. I need hardly say that my first wife was the best of the lot, an intelligent woman who disappeared immediately after our divorce and whom I've never been able to relocate. Yes, there was some news that she'd been seen in Colorado, in that mountainous part where it were just about impossible to find a person as short as she. I give her credit, too, for her patience, her familiarity with the Latin American postal history prior to World War II, and her physique when she was naked, which was only too seldom the case. I don't know what happened to us. Unless it was her preference for the Classical era over the Romantic in music history. What I can tell you is that we used to take walks on moonlit nights. And that's all I can say on that topic, lest I break down into tears just talking about it. She had an odd hat and an old-fashioned brown dress designed seemingly for nineteenth-century farmwives. And yes, that was another of my weaknesses, matching as it did my kerosene lamps, my Victorian novels, and the button-up shoes that have caused so much merriment at my place of work. But enough concerning her and her decision to leave me to deal unassisted with my personal quiddities, which are no fault of mine.

She used to bring home dogs, and even on one occasion a grounded grackle of some description. Give her back to me, and I'll happily attend to every injured bird within a hundred miles.

My second wife followed hard upon. She was only some two inches taller than the first one, but even so wasn't interested in using the clothes left behind by Gwen. And this was just the first in a whole series of superstitions and extravagancies on her part. Curtains, a new tablecloth. I made no comment on these matters, however, not till she began dipping into her paycheck for clothes and doodads, a Navaho pot, and just a month after our wedding, a shopping trip to a store of some sort out on Long Island.

My third wife made an excellent presentation, was neat and tidy at all times, and had a degree from a school in Missouri, as she claimed. Not till two weeks had gone by did she admit finally that the university was in fact located in Massachusetts. We continued on all the same, staying together for nearly a year before I fully understood that beneath the grooming and toiletries and her prosperous job, the woman had bitten deeply, very deeply indeed, into the feminist philosophy. In any case she had cared next to nothing for philatelic matters and when pressed, admitted she didn't detest New York City.

Thus ended my associations with women, saving only a five-week connection with a Brooklyn woman full of lipstick and earrings and an accent that left my auditory faculties permanently damaged.

On December 19, there was a clear night, cold outside but exceedingly cozy inside the house. Going to the cabinet, I took out my Czechoslovak album and turned immediately to perhaps one of the most plangent scenes in the Europe of that day. A man of obvious genius, the engraver had managed to portray a mile or two of perspective within a .426-square inch frame that also held a peasant's cottage in the extreme distance with smoke lifting from the chimney. One of the windows was aglow, and I almost believed for a moment that I could detect the householder himself playing on a violin in front of the fireplace. But no, it was just my abnormal imagination again, the one that had already destroyed three marriages and a perfectly good arrangement with a girl from Sheepshead Bay.

It must have been late fall or early winter in Czechoslovakia on that stamp, to reckon by the mown fields and leaves on the ground. Overripe pumpkins decaying forlornly on the stem, a child swinging from a limb. Pleased by everything that I could see, I lifted the stamp from the sheet and after checking both doors, transported the little artifact to the adjoining room, where my microscope and chemicals were stored. It was a Lithuanian-made product, this instrument of mine, and extorted a good deal of patience to get the focus just right. Again I scanned the stubble, the stars and smoke, the broken roof tile, and the illuminated front room wherein the imagined peasant had lately been standing. At one time the whole world had been like this.

Come 3:07, I left the desk and initiated the five steps that took me to the window. They were diligent enough certainly, the pullulating brown immigrants working night after night on the wall. A parabolic structure, the thing had originally been intended to sequester a certain ten-block set-aside that the police nowadays demurred to enter. Fetching my telescope, I made what probably would be my last inspection of that dread district that lapped my own neighborhood and came to within a few rods of an outdoor marketplace where Caucasian foods were still on offer. Further I could see some dozen or more mile-high towers flashing urgent messages out to ships at sea. Upon these, too, I trained my telescope, especially a lilac-colored lamp of great wattage that just then ceased to function, the filament having no doubt exhausted itself.

I am not insane. It happens merely that I love my leisure, my coffee, my dog, books, and particularly my seventeen-volume stamp collection spilling over with art and history while offering a pathway to better times. I would long ago have surrendered to a lifetime of solitary confinement, provided I had a blanket, a pee pot, and could keep my collection with me.

It was just past four in the morning when I abandoned my bed and returned to the table. I had left the stamp in its position, but the microscope had again to be adjusted in order to account, I suppose, for the rotation of the Earth and sunspot activity over the interval. Obviously there was no "peasant with a violin" to be seen, although the outlying fields remained as perfectly mown and moonlit as before. That was when I shifted to the northwest corner of the scene, and after making a final adjustment, almost fell to the floor, aghast to find an infinitesimal boy standing up to his waist in the stubble while waving back in friendly fashion from about a hundred years ago.

Ten

I have come upon these pages, and must consider whether to continue with them or not.

Eleven

I have chosen to continue with these pages, if only that I may be seen doing something in the eyes of my superiors [*sic*]. But I should remark that my desk, formerly near the front of the second row, has been moved to the back of the room, a promotion in my mind but a demotion in theirs. Certainly they dare not dismiss me, not with my popularity among these thirty-one standard-issue colleagues who admire my virtues and character, my self-presentation, my courtesies to women, my tolerant approach to things, and the infectious good humor I contribute to our little group. Truth is, I need just seventeen months and a few days till I can claim my pension at eighty-two percent of the full rate. Let them try to fire me at this date, and the whole city would rise up in hot indignation and forward-looking self-interest.

My contempt was growing, and my reanimated *camera obscura* (computer) could now do all sorts of things it oughtn't. On Tuesday I invested a good, or rather a bad, five minutes looking by remote sensing into a randomly-chosen home in Jersey, a place with three television sets, and on the bedside table a bottle of sleeping pills, a glass with something in it, and a novel such as might give pleasure to the *New York Times*. Of the beds, one was unmade, but the other wasn't. The kitchen, I admit, was neat and tidy, but had two sentimental landscapes on the wall and a hagiographic rendering of JFK on the refrigerator door. Next, I pulled up the hologram of a large building in Pakistan with people coming in and out. As for my own residence, the lawn needed work, and through the window I could see the back of my own poor head bending over my collection. Thankfully, there was nothing else in that room (apart from a hand-colored print of last century's pre-eminent philatelist) to excite even the most belligerent agents of the State's Housing, Rehabilitation, and Gratification Department. Indeed, the day was drawing on, and thus far I had succeeded in doing nothing that could contribute to the present system.

By 11:24, I had fallen into a hypnagogic state in which I imagined myself sailing a gilded ocean made of glass. My memory reverted then to a certain Salvadorian commemorative of 1949 that pictured the sea exactly as I featured it. That was when I became aware of the organization's lead proctor standing just at my side, a tall woman, well dressed, urging me with quickly declining patience to take the day's mandated medications.

I did as required and then yawned and stretched so as to appear unaware of the newly-hired bozo smiling in my direction. The noon hour was drawing near, and now this new ignoramus probably wished, like so many others, to contract a discussion with the company's premier intellect. For him, that would represent a promotion, for me a wasted hour. After so many years on the job, I was tired, tired unto the absolute death of having to pretend that I wasn't even more exceptional than they knew, an indigo bunting amongst jays and wrens.

Eschewing the elevator, I managed to climb to the thirty-fourth floor, where one of the better and less visited restrooms proved uninhabited at this time. With my own toilet out of commission, I needs take full advantage when I can. And then, too, someone had left behind—don't expect me to describe it—a pornographic watercolor of the highest quality. The custodian here, a friend of mine and the only person I know destined for paradise, had declined to erase the thing.

I read, briefly, a few pages in Cockayne's *Leechdoms, Wortcunning, and Starcraft* while taking a few swills betimes of sweetened brandy wine. Entered then one of the thirty-fourth-floor people who began very briskly washing his hands. He was whistling a tune, a poor one, and I could see his shoes under the partition. The feet were small and yet his rubber soles so compressed that I figured him for a fat person. Worse, he seemed to have a living insect of some nature peeping over the edge of his nearer cuff. We looked at each other.

The streets were bleak and cold and the rest of that. High winds bending great buildings to the breaking point. Amazingly, I hadn't gone a full block before I descried that same pair of shoes marching side by side with me. He was, the owner of that footwear, quite as heavy as I had foreseen, and yet his profile (elongated by action of the low winter Sun) was not as loathsome as it so well might have been. The champion in that category was a uniformed Pinkerton standing on the corner with a beet-red face.

I have read where old Leland Pefley once escaped into a Christian Science Reading Room when in similar circumstances. Bad for me, all that I could see was a congeries of public benches in that two-acre park that abuts upon 19th Street. Each bench bore an inch of urban snow, a granular material that hadn't stopped an inebriated and shirtless New Yorker from seating himself there while reading out in a loud voice the stock quotations from a discarded sheet of newspaper that proved, as I drew near, to be about two weeks old.

I still had twenty-one minutes left to me, a concession to my seniority with the Department. The day was sixty-two percent finished while my career was advancing even faster than that. With that in mind, I came to my forty-story bank building, sustained by my after-tax deposits of $3,600 monthly, more or less. (More *or* less? If my deposits were sometimes more, it stands to reason they must sometimes be less, for Christ's sakes.) Twenty feet above me, I spied a gargoyle dressed in a wig of pigeon manure. But in all truth, it really was a friendly locale for doing business, where the automation was loaded with pleasant voices always ready to apologize.

There was a reverential atmosphere in that building, all of it presided over by an enormous Pinkerton blocking the exit. As a person who could do many things at once, his left hand kept opening and closing around the handle of his government-supplied baton. The West might rise, the West might fall, a destiny that fluctuated with the transactions taking place here among a computer array.

Not that I despised my own poor share of wealth. I used to withdraw a few bills and carry them into one of the private booths where I could sniff at the stuff in peace. Each hundred dollars represented four hours of future freedom. It's an ugly sort of specie, of course, bearing the portraits of men that never certainly would have been chosen by me. Poe, where was he? Lee Harvey Oswald? Tito Perdue? John Wilkes Booth?

I don't always know the sum of my own holdings, an elusive quotient that oscillates with market conditions. Today all things were looking good—housing starts were up, and Moldova was back in the market for American debt. I lifted a twenty-dollar bill from the safe box in front of me, and after fitting on my glasses, proofed the famous prose—"Buy low, sell high"—that bears the endorsement of the nation's Treasurer, a haunted man, as his calligraphy seems to suggest. I thought of tying a thread to that bill and trailing it along behind me as I walked. Would my third wife come chasing after and ask to have me back?

At present I have just $220,000 in bonds at maturity value, and rather less than that in equities and cash money, a decent sum in my father's day but scarcely enough today for groceries, stamps, utilities, and dog feed. I realized then that I had been talking to myself, reckoning by all the people watching from across the floor. At that point I decided to return my money and my half-dozen most pricy stamps to the metal box, a grey thing eight times longer than wide, return it to the "cave" in the wall that continued on for an unfathomable distance before coming out presumably at the other end.

I bowed to the clerks, smiled, and left the building. Keeping my attention on the shoes and socks that drifted into ken, I espied a penny that no one had troubled to collect. Me, I wanted it, and later on was deeply abashed for having failed to pick it up in the admittedly heavy traffic. Even just a penny can buy a microsecond of retirement time.

I entered my place of work in the guise of an avuncular sort of middle-aged person with a limp.

"Haven't lost a penny, have you?" I asked the wom-

an in the first row, a worried-looking quantity in a
grey skirt that fell partway to the floor. "If so, I know
where it is."

"A penny?" (No sense of humor. Nor of sense itself.)

"Why, yes. Where's there one, there might be others."

She went back to work. Of all the women, she was
the one who most readily saw through my preten-
sions. I reached out to tickle her under the chin but
changed my mind when I bethought me of recent
laws bearing on that activity.

Twelve

Is it possible to write a whole book in which nothing ever happens? Pefley did it. But then he was one
of those who cares only for what goes on in the mind,
and nothing at all for what a person does with his
hands. Indeed, it was said of him that he had himself
at one time tickled a woman under the chin.

I went up to 38th Street, turned eastward, refusing
to look into the anguished faces of New Yorkers always asking the same question. "Is this what life is
for?" And: "I'm rich, but dare I leave town while
someone might steal my accounts?" And: "I'm not so
old. Heck, I still have time for at least two more di-
vorces!"

And then turned right when I came to Lavrenti Avenue, a narrow conduit named after a historical per-
sonage. Here were all sorts of boutiques and cozy little shops specializing in quaint little objects devoid of
value. I halted here for longer than I should, regaling
myself with the sight of upper-class woman ecstasiz-

ing over the junk. For thirty years, no drop of rain or
heat of summer had been allowed to touch any of
these persons. The day *was* overcast, however, and it
was perhaps too soon to give up hope. In dreams of
total destruction, I see great balls of fire tumbling
down from Yonkers.

By 5:38 I had arrived at the hundred-and-fifty-year-
old hall that once had served for cattle auctions in the
Agrarian Age. Gathered here were the finest people to
be found anywhere, coin and stamp collectors drawn
from as far as Europe, if not even further indeed. A
smiling Chinese was standing behind a glass counter
in which his country's postal history was gorgeously
displayed. Trembling, I drew out a cigarette, but
promptly put it back again when I recollected how
this was the worst of places in which to indulge my
vice. If it were absolutely necessary to live in New
York City in order to attend these exhibitions, then I
must goddamn it live in New York City. Or come once
in a while on visits.

To begin, I drifted toward the East European dis-
plays. I do love that region, where so many ideological
experiments are forever being carried out. I mention
Romania, a land that rotates from royalism to fascism
to Communism and back again. In a place like that,
one always has a chance to see his own utopia have its
turn at last. (Me, I'll vote for any government that
promises to bring people closer to transcendence
through the viaduct of beauty.) And then, too, no
other country has more courageously resisted the
prosperity that has so degraded the remaining parts of
Europe.

In this gallery, someone had tediously and labori-
ously set out five series of pre-war stamps comprising
some of my favorite issues. But hadn't seen half the

display, I had not, before my better eye—it was here I took out my glasses and put them on—before that eye lit upon the noble image of Corneliu Codreanu standing somewhat apart from the mass of other Romanian heroes. Yes, I had three copies of that stamp already; even so, I wanted to build a personal monopoly of that issue and then sell them later on at great profit to the patriots of the future.

I approached the saleslady, an insensitive-looking entity munching on a foodstuff of some nature. Her face was splotched, and I divined in her the sort of personality that could become extraordinarily angry on very short notice. Other characteristics combined in such a way as to encourage me to retreat from her presence and float further down the aisle to Hungary, where a knot of unseemly-looking and unsmiling men were debating about something or another in that "language" of theirs. Truth is, I have especially admired this race of men, based upon their elevated suicide rate. The most counter-intuitive of actions, it represents the triumph of thought over instinct. It was just then that the men stopped talking and then turned and looked at me for a long time in unbroken silence.

I returned to Romania and the woman. She had finished with solid foods and now was drawing upon a potbellied bottle with something in it.

"How much," I asked, "for the Codreanu?"

She began to get angry. I went on:

"Maybe so, maybe so. But we must judge these matters *aesthetically*, what? And put politics off to one side?"

Her reply, based visibly on the Romance languages, was as awful as anything that could be heard in that cave-like place, excluding neither Hungarian, Chi-

nese, nor the local speech. Exasperated beyond everything, I reached out and lay my finger on the actual
stamp. That did it; right away a burly man whom I
had been stupid enough to ignore came up and
nudged me back to Hungary once again.

The world is full of stamps, and stamps are full of
the world, provided only a person knows how to see
them aright. Buildings, fish, dictators, wild roses with
bees in them, why should anyone go on actual travels?
I get better views of the Hagia Sophia than those who
go there at great expense in order to stand in line for a
chance at the restroom. On stamps I have seen into
the face of Pythagoras, as good a view certainly as ever
his wife procured. I have seen much, all the human
nations from best to worst. But most of all I have an
affinity for stamps with maps on them. I own one of
these, a Syrian imprint showing a great empty space
of which nothing was then known. I could imagine
myself trudging forward for days, sand in my shoes,
nothing whatsoever coming into view. And then there
are those stamps that give pictures of other stamps,
and so to infinity. I tend to shy away from these.

I want it on record that I unloaded more than $215
in this place, most of it going for Baltic issues. I
should also mention that one of the world's very
greatest collections had been brought here on loan
from Lucknow and a portion of it set up in glass cases.
We wandered among these wonders, the other collectors and me, all of us suffering from envy and greed
and excess of beauty arranged all too sumptuously
before our eyes. I admired the man at my side who
had thought to bring a child's telescope by means of
which he could inspect the stamps as nearly as a jew-
eler. Seeing the anguish in my face, the man turned
and:

"Care to borrow this? Look at that four-penny black in the green binder."

I accepted the offer and looked at the suggested item, a soot-colored thing devoid of beauty that however had fetched $217,000 at the San Francisco auction. Me, I value beauty, beauty only, beauty every day.

"May I?" the man asked. "Have my telescope back?"

Seen at five times real size, his face looked like a sheet of rubber with burnt places for mouths and eyes. I judged him at about my own age, give or take some half-score of years. And yes, he did have that tortured look that characterizes your garden-variety stamp, coin, or beer can collector.

"Just one minute, please," said I, holding on to the instrument. I had acquired the view of a pretty girl in whom that strange area just behind the knee was visible. There's a serious artery that feeds that area, although not one always visible under a cursory inspection. Another few inches, one might have seen where her hosiery, assuming she had any, comes to a stop before getting embroiled with her maiden hair.

"Please?"

I returned him his field glasses. He was, or rather is, a bit too tall for the distribution of his weight. Even so I wouldn't care to tangle with him, not after having witnessed in my youth the sort of damage these types can inflict. This one had wounded himself shaving and bore a tad of toilet paper adhering to his chin. I liked him. Or rather didn't detest him all at once, which for me amounts to the same.

"You speak of that four-penny. Fact is, I have the plate block."

"You don't!"

"I do. But hardly ever allow anyone to see it."

We moved diplomatically through the crowd, keeping well away from a minor riot that had broken out at the Afghani booth. A gun show was in progress in a lateral wing of the building, the two different sorts of attendees also keeping away from each other. Outside (where else?) it was snowing again, an unwelcome development for people without the proper clothing. We walked hurriedly along the storefronts, putting ourselves insofar as possible in the shade of the awnings, where we had to contend with other people in debt to our example. Thus came into view the whole cornucopia of the country's products, services, and merchandise. Women's shops especially; I passed twenty of these as against a single bookstore, which in the event had gone out of business.

"Notice how the snow is being driven into our eyes," I said, receiving no reply. The fellow was carrying a portmanteau with him, a slim one made of reptile skin. I was prepared to wager half of everything I had that it held either stamps, coins, beer cans, or cash.

"Stamps," he said.

"Well! Let's have a look at 'em!"

"Here? In all this snow? Hell no."

"Ah, so? Well, if not now, when?"

"When we get to your place! That *is* where we're going, isn't it?"

"I thought we were going with you! Cheez. However, it's true that I have a stamp room. Temperature controlled. And a long flat table and bright lights to see with, you understand."

"Yes, I supposed you might have those things. Most of us do, after all." Just then he stopped and began pointing around in all directions at the city itself, a highly eminent domain that lay like a swamp below us. Except that those were houses and homes instead of the phosphorescence seen in your typical swamps. "There must be *tens of thousands* of flat tables in this city. And so that part I can believe."

I said no more at that juncture. My dog was waiting. Meantime, a fire had broken out in the direction of Queens, an aptly-named borough famous for its hairdressers. Fire and snow, money and noise, and the silent deaths now taking place with actuarial precision in the encompassing apartment houses.

"Gives me the creeps."

"Well, of course."

"Better to be reaping wheat under the Sun, as in that wonderful Hungarian series."

"Oh, Lord. You can get all those you want for about a penny apiece."

Again we stopped, this time so I could light his cigarette. In the flame, his face was seen to be a good deal worse than I had at first allowed.

"Veteran, are you? The Bolivian mess?"

"No, no. Ha. No, spent seventeen years in the futures trading pit."

"And so you're rich, then."

"Was. Until soybeans went against me."

"They'll do that."

"Lost three mil in five minutes."

"Baal! That's . . . what? Six hundred Gs a minute?"

"Don't remind me."

My heart went out to him. And now he was reduced to peddling stamps out of a lorn briefcase with some of the original snake scales still clinging to it.

We hesitated for a minute as the dog reviewed the man's socks and crotch. I had hoped the dishes would have been washed by now, but the dog was a good deal older than he used to be. One single saucer lay upside down on the counter, the contents gone.

"Tea?" I asked my visitor. "Or coffee?"

"Daiquiri. And don't be parsimonious with the vodka."

"I use rum."

"Coffee, then."

His legs were as long as stilts but tended to vanish when he was in the seated position. He had an intellectual forehead, somewhat intellectual, and had tried to make himself presentable. We now commenced to make ready to begin looking at the man's stamps. His album, too, had been covered in the same sort of skin (taken perhaps from the same armadillo), as covered his valise. He moved deftly, suggesting he was as familiar with the album and its contents as with all the other things he was likely to be familiar with. He opened to "Iran," so-called, a name with far fewer historical associations than "Persia," a more poetic nomenclature by far. My mind flew back to Achemenian times, the tomb of Cyrus, the expedition of the Ten Thousand, and so on. And yet the stamps he showed were simple counterfeits, as I could easily discern even without resorting to my magnifying glass.

"Yes," I said. "Some people specialize in those, forgeries."

He blushed. "Forgeries! I hadn't realized! Okay, I can let you have them at a discount."

"That's real white of you. Actually, I don't even want them in my house."

"No. Nor do I. Should I take them outside?"

I waved it away. He might have some good stuff in that album, peculiarities with landscape scenes, BOBs, airmails, and above all hand-cancelled beauties from some of the poorest countries on Earth. This is what I mostly wanted. I have invested in stamps that, some of them, must have carried love letters to pre-postmodern girls waiting eagerly in the Barbados. I am especially proud of my 1930 2 c. Uruguayan Pegasus that bears a five-word handwritten message in minuscule print. Were only it not illegible, the history of Uruguay might have turned out better. Impatient to set eyes on further examples, I took the man's album over into my two best hands and turned quickly to the Barbados themselves. Not forgeries. Well pleased, I bent nearer and then ran for the nine-inch magnification glass that had come down to me from my fathers. Not that my immediate father had done much to enhance the collection.

"You have some pretty good material here," I admitted.

"Pretty good? No, sir."

"OK, *very* good."

"That's better. Actually, I would have preferred real coffee, percolated, as opposed to this . . . what? Anhydrous stuff?"

"I have always loved the Newfoundland postage. Hell, I'd be willing to pay up to, say, a couple hundred for these 1932 issues."

He laughed, and soon I had to join him. That lot was worth well more than a thousand dollars to any fair-minded buyer. "Alright, how about five hundred? Five hundred golden-green American dollars hot off the press?"

He laughed. His teeth were poor, especially the more eminent ones, while the tongue itself had a saurian aspect that incited me to look away.

"Very well," I continued stubbornly. "We need to be honest. Give you seven-fifty for the decade. That's three-fourths of a thousand dollars, you understand."

He laughed no more. Instead, he took back the album, overcoming without much difficulty the little bit of resistance I might have tried. His next ploy was to move toward the door, which I had predicted, however.

"Turn the knob to the right," I called. "Turn it to the left and nothing will come of that."

"What about the dog?"

"No, no, he doesn't harm people who are leaving. Only those who . . ."

"Are entering?"

"You're smart. Smart about dogs and smart about stamps. And I just realized I don't even know your name."

"Not Jones and not Smith. What else you need to know?"

He was certifiably a philatelist, this guest of mine, and like most such people had given up on barbers, haberdashers, cobblers, and dentists. It came to me that he might soon be dead, judging from the violence of his tremors when speaking of stamps.

"Who will inherit your collection, I wonder? No, I'm just asking."

His voice was weak at that distance. The walls, full of insulation, tended rather to absorb sounds than to send them on their way.

"Have no children," he said, speaking yet more weakly. "And, of course, lost my wife along with my shares."

"Where is she now?"

"In Detroit with some guy. Big collection, bigger than mine."

"Say, I've just now had an odd thought. Or slightly odd, anyway. What, for example, if I were to bequeath you my collection, and you me? One of us would end up with a lot of really good material, what?"

He thought. His skin was not altogether unlike that of his briefcase and suggested he might be afflicted with one of the new diseases. He replied: "You're not exactly a model of perfect health yourself, are you?"

"Health? It's been years since I had any of that. So we agree?"

"I suppose not. And besides, I haven't even seen your collection."

"I have six volumes in East Europe alone."

"Ah. You've never actually been there, I take it."

"As for Hungary, I have a good ninety-eight percent of the entire pre-war issuance!"

"The Wakefield Collection has them all."

"So I've been made to understand. Gad. Sure would like to get my hands on some of that stuff."

"Yes, and they had just two single policemen on guard. Careless, careless."

"Just think what a person could do with one of those little digital glass cutters."

"Or by climbing in through the chimney. Say, why don't you turn loose of that knob and take a seat, for Christ's sakes? I'm tired of yelling."

"Once inside, a man could take the whole bloody collection!"

"Baal!"

"Precisely."

Thirteen

In fact he spent three full days in the basement, did my guest, long enough to survey my collection and make a series of negative, neutral, and positive comments regarding it. I had never much cared for my Central American accumulation, an all-too-utilitarian output with its predictable images and inferior inks. My guest, on the other hand, adored that section and could sometimes be heard groaning in the basement, along with other sounds indicative of a medical condition. And all this time it had continued to snow in New York City, a heaven-sent anodyne to cover the hideousness of the place.

It displeased me to have an oddball sleeping in my house, which is not even to mention the dog's reaction. I would go to work, come home at noon to check on my collection, and then fly back to the office, all in less than two hours or less. Meantime with great effort, I had managed with the aid of my rehabilitated computer to retrieve a blueprint of the building where the stamp auction was still progressing. Such diagrams are required for purposes of fire insurance, don't you see, and offer all sorts of wonderful information for people willing to seek it. But when I visited the nearest hardware and asked for the least expensive set of diamond-tipped glasscutters, the son-of-a-bitch wanted to see my driver's license (long expired), my DNA hologram, my security clearance, and the half-dozen billfold-size photographs of my wives.

"She's the hottest," he said, bringing the picture of my worst wife up to his eye. "What, did she abandon you or something?"

"I abandoned *her!*"

"Sure, you did. Anyway, you don't need no stinking glass cutters. 'Less you got some sort of mischief in mind. Do you?"

I looked to heaven in exasperation, but then finally strove to bribe the man with one of the new twenty-five-dollar bills bearing the image of The Reverend Martin Luther King on it. Junior, I ought have said. A bald man with tattoos forming two supernumerary eyes, the salesindividual gathered the thing, got into his glasses, jotted down the serial number, and then dropped it into a former milk bottle that held a fair number of other dubious bills. Which of those four eyes of his were actually viable? To this day I cannot with assurance say.

"Oh, goodie!" he exclaimed. "Now I can get that operation!"

I produced two more bills of the same quality and let them fall (like autumn leaves they seemed) to the counter, where they landed in different places. I reached out better to organize them, but before I could get there, both had disappeared!

"You need to read the instructions," the blighter said as he removed the instrument from its package and pointed to the wee little diamonds, none of them larger than a really very tiny thing. Was it indeed so delicate, that apparatus, that it needed so much protective material?

"You have to lubricate it with this here 'naphtha,' we call it," (he produced the naphtha), "or elsewise she's liable to get too hot. Shit, some of those windows is three inches thick, for Pete's sake!"

I took the product, thanked the gentleman, and scurried back to the office in time to use the restroom. A long time I sat there, warding off the temptation to experiment aforetimes with the rather odd-looking product that had cost so much.

Fourteen

My retirement draws nearer, and already my employer and I have begun to celebrate. With just seven

weeks to go, I was given a fancy all-weather barome-
ter that upon first inspection appeared to be unused.
Having put on my best face and utmost charm, I
thanked the two wonderful women who had presented me it. One was fat and the other thin, and between
the both of them they formed a more or less normal
presentation. To reciprocate I picked up two pieces of
simulated jewelry at a junk shop where by good hap I
came across one of Perdue's lesser-known works.
Compared to the master of the craft, how dare I go on
putting words on paper?

But readers are more interested in my glass cutter
and quondam houseguest. Truth is, we plotted and
planned over the course of three full days and nights,
but by the time we had screwed up our courage, the
divine collection had been taken down and sent back
to its owner in Lucknow. Thus ended my last reason-
able hope of completing the Chinese and Korean sec-
tors of my collection. My guest departed shortly after,
and apart from some four or five occasions, I was never to hear from him again. He had learned to do forgeries himself and had met a woman who, unlike any
wives of mine, was highly willing to assist with coun-
terfeiting high-value stamps of the German states. I
have to assume that he has died by now, or will do so
in the future, reckoning from the tenor of his letters. I
remain grateful to him for having returned one of my
most precious stamps, purloined by him on the second day of his visit. Three others of the same vintage
continue to be missing.

She sleeps now (picking up where I left off above regarding my second wife) in a progressive cemetery on the outskirts of the city alongside the poly-gendered pedophile who had been her next-to-last husband. Her last months, I learned, had been happy ones granting full satisfaction in all her orifices. I confess that I did actually contribute $1000 to her last marriage, wanting it to last.

Fifteen

Time goes by, sometimes quickly and sometimes quite the other way around. Me, I proceed at a more or less typical pace toward old age, senility, and the possibility of the world's fifth-best accumulation of Austro-Hungarian *tête-bêches*. Day by day I am more and more alone, moving from strength to strength as I immerse myself deeper and deeper into books, stamps, and music, democracy's most rueful enemies. When alone, I often reenact historical parts and sometimes venture out at night to watch pods of whale-like clouds migrating through the sky.

And then on the ninth day after that, I was visited by two city officials responding to a report that my home had been abandoned and uncollected mail was accumulating on the porch. Well, we had a good laugh about that, which is to say till the tall one with the diamond in his nose perceived I was carrying half a package of exposed cigarettes in my pocket.

"Are you a smoking man? Sir?"

"Ha! Smoking. I did used to be, that's for sure."

"How about now?"

"Now? But I never smoke when I'm driving at the same time."

There followed a brief silence, briefer even than the time needed to mention it. Suddenly the other man, the one with a plug in his ear and a brief antenna sticking out behind, lurched forward and began to climb the stairs. Nor was I allowed to follow.

"There's nothing up there, actually," I called after him. "Just a bunch of old books and whatnot."

"'Old books?' And these books, as you call them, do they tell you what happens to a person's lungs? When you smoke cigarettes in enclosed places? Where innocent people are present? I thought not."

"And unenclosed, too," the other man said. Just then, seeing that I was staring at his revolver, he dropped back two spaces.

"I wouldn't know how to fire it anyway," I said, smiling betimes. "What is that, a .38?"

"Just keep your hands where I can see them, okay?"

I agreed to it. "Anyway," said I, "I've been thinking that really I ought to give up on cigarettes. The costs, don't you know. And *odor*! Yuk."

The first man now returned to us, holding between his thumb and finger a superannuated paperback of Conrad's *Nigger of the Narcissus*.

"Well, lookie here," he said. "There's just no telling what you might find. If you know where to look."

It was on the night after that I drifted up Third Avenue to my personal theatre, New York's most dilapidated building. Here, roaches gamboled in freedom, fattening themselves on residues of chewing gum. But here, too, was where old-fashioned black-and-white films from the '40s and '50s could still be viewed, a boon for those of us sick to death of watching subhumans congressing at high magnification in front of our eyes.

My special place was in the nineteenth row, far from the alcoholics sleeping in the front and retrophile film students congregated in the back. One single individual had chosen to sit in front of me, though I was soon able to send him on his way by means of simulated smoke from my analog cigarette. With some minutes before the show was to start, I began to dream that it was also 1940 or '50 in the outer world. My excitement increased. Very soon I would be entering a dimension in which romance had priority over coitus, where people spoke English, men wore suits, and the themes were serious. Had ever such a world really existed?

Sixteen

Continually more awful are my dreams. Last night again, to take only the most recent example, I imagined I was fighting with my middle wife. A red-headed bitch with roots in Ireland, she had been trying for years to promote me in the eyes of society. I suppose I must have attended a dozen parties in pursuance of her ambition, until driven to despair she made herself into an "entrepreneur" and squandered half my savings on a boutique in Brooklyn specializing in nasty underwear.

I dreamt that I had thrown her down the stairwell, a solution old Schopenhauer had pioneered with a similar female. Of stamps themselves, she had cared only for the cheerful ones, modern garbage picturing butterflies and spaceships, and in one notorious case, Mickey Mouse himself.

"What's the good of these things," she asked about my stamps, her upper lip curled in her accustomed way. That would be the moment I ought have tossed her down the stairwell.

"'What good? What good?" I cleverly replied. And then, after allowing my riposte to sink in: "And what good are *you*, so far as that goes?"

She wept, the first time in over a week. "I'm a human being!"

"By God, I believe you've put your finger on it!"

"I don't even know why you married me!"

"Sex. But I could have done better with a jar of cold mayonnaise."

Sometimes her tears would turn to laughter. But not that day. Not with the four children—just one of them, the worst of the lot, was mine—watching worriedly from the balcony. And yet, the bitch had borne other fruits almost as rotten. The eldest girl, initiated to lesbianism by television, shaved her head and carried a ten-inch switchblade. I kept well away from her. And then there was Leroy, a tall individual fathered by a black person never to be seen again. The third child, worse even than mine, had left school at fifteen after having already established an unlicensed enterprise involving pharmaceuticals transported from Honduras.

I now choose to end this effort to account for my latter years. Farewell.

Seventeen

But instead of sons and daughters, it was the little neighboring boy I found waiting on my front porch. (I have decided to continue this narration of mine, never ask me why.) He had somehow climbed the fence and had worked his way through the downed trees that were to keep people from my door and had planted himself on the top step with his wretched little stamp album grasped in his unclean hands.

"Hi," he succinctly said.

"You!"

"Want to trade stamps?"

We went in. The boy could drink more chocolate milk than the combined 1943 Russo-American armies swilling in tandem. Seated just across from him in dim light, the dog and I waited in silence till the milk was gone. Of all the little boys in all the deteriorating houses in all New York, why couldn't *he* have been my son as opposed to the one that was? Trade stamps? Far rather had I traded boys.

"How's your schoolwork going, Feenie?"

"I got some new stamps from Argentina. Want to trade? One of 'em's red."

"Well, let's see what you've got there. Sounds real good."

What he had there was a little 3 x 5 glassine envelope holding perhaps a dozen Argentine commemoratives of minimum value.

"Interesting. By the way, I've got some doughnuts in the kitchen."

"No, thanks. The red one's got a woman on it."

"A *naked* woman?"

He looked at me severely, then stood suddenly and started to leave.

"Okay, I'll trade you five green stamps for just one red one."

He sat back down. His album was thin and miserable and had no more than a couple hundred poorly mounted commonplace items in it.

"You need to use *hinges*, Feenie, when you mount those things. Glue is bad and damages the album."

"Naw, it don't matter. I'll be finished with this particular phase pretty soon, anyway."

I looked at him. His head was a tetrahedral with a bump on top. His arms were spindly and had barely the strength to support the combined weight of his fingers and hands. His legs did reach the ground, concluding in two feet housed in shoes that were identical in all ways save in color and size. His eyes meanwhile (and here was the problem) were all times focused on the ground.

"What do you see down there, partner?"

"Nothing. Things."

Of doughnuts, I collect those only as have frosting on them. Having nudged the platter closer to the boy, he refused to look at it.

"What would you do, Feenie, if someone left you a lot of money?"

"I don't know. Buy a dog."

"Like *my* dog?"

"Naw. How much you want for him?"

"Hundred dollars."

"Naw. Can't afford it."

"Well, how much can you afford?"

"I don't know. I got five shares my grandmother gave me."

"Shares of stock?"

"Yeah."

"Well! You can pay me out of dividends."

"Okay. Say, where'd you get all these stamps, that's what I want to know. I don't have any like this one."

His taste, like mine, was for gaudy things. Working with exaggerated carefulness, I lifted the stamp with my bespoken tongs and passed it over to him in such a way that he must extend his ridiculous arm quite a long distance way in order to retrieve it.

"You'll have to feed him every day. And water."

"Yeah. I don't even have any like this one, either," he said, touching with his blunt finger a mint stamp with the picture of a vampire on it.

Eighteen

I woke at ten, nonplussed to find that I was in the early evening of my late middle age. Contrary to all my hopes, it was *not* the weekend, and now, bringing my Will into play, I threw my persona out of bed and, after micturating in the appointed place, got into the same set of clothes I had worn on that day two months ago when I had arrived at work earlier than normal. I was congratulated for coming at all. My behavior and laziness had so developed in recent weeks that obviously I must enjoy the support of some very important person—this is what they believed.

I had stayed up late drinking wine and working on my collection, the proximate cause, I believe, why every day my colleagues were more and more coming to resemble my fourth-grade teacher, an earnest and hard-working woman who had done great intellectual damage to the children she so clearly loved. But now back to present time—the woman just to my right was less like my old-time teacher than my uncle on my mother's side, a slit-eyed personality who once had used a stamp of mine for postage.

I must drink no more wine at night, or not until my retirement. I must also apply myself to my work, must gather more and more non-public information from foreign sources, must stop smoking, must leave off comparing my fellow workers to protozoa. Accordingly, I turned on my computer and, after allowing time for it to accept my codeword and DNA, began right away downloading protected information on dental hygiene in the Central African Republic. An uncouth language, the translation required more than the usual time. I would have liked a cigarette; instead, rising and stretching and going to the window and examining the tableau seven hundred feet below me, I saw me a sight that put me into the worst depression in seven hundred days.

There, so far away, I saw a couple rush into each other's arms and stand there embracing for a full half-minute or more, a longer time than most people realize. And how long, pray, before any similar woman would wish to come into *my* arms, what?, and remain there for a parallel length of time? Never happen, not at my age, never again, though the world go on forever without end. Or until my first wife recognize her errors and come running home again. Not that I wasn't also at some fault, especially that day I struck her a time or two, too hard perhaps, for mixing up the imperforates in my Near Eastern collection. However, I suppose she's as old as me by now, that she has had children, and that her beauty has eroded into something as disappointing as that of ordinary bell-curve women who have no real interest in philatelic matters.

That wouldn't be her down there, the woman I was watching? Clinging to that most fortunate of all husbands? Husband and wife embracing each other in shared happiness after a successful morning at the stamp and coin shops? Not likely. The city has nine million monads in it, and it was beyond impossible that I could have found the one good person in all that mess. Ridiculous. Even so, I got up quickly and was about to run to the elevator when the woman in the next-door cubicle spoke up loud and clear: "Leaving us again?" she asked.

"Yes," I confessed, putting on a serious and even a spiritual expression. "I need to visit the Reverend Martin Luther King Jr. Memorial Array, the one on 88th Street."

"Oh."

There were very few people using the elevator at this time, and I was able to choose my own side of that conveyance, exposing only a very partial silhouette. The other passenger was as grumpy as me, and we seemed to be in the first stages of an unvoiced compact based on shared attributes. Were only the whole world like that, with mutual understanding everywhere! We fell past the fourth floor, given a hasty view of a laughing woman with a mouth full of luminescent silver fillings fore and aft.

"Dumb bitch," said my traveling companion.

"Right. Redhead, too."

We came to ground at precisely 10:08 and, like civilized people everywhere, went our separate ways. There was a good bright Sun outside, the sort that urges a person to go out into the countryside and take a long stroll with himself or his divorced woman. It urged me in particular to lie face-up in a little rowboat drifting at hazard on an idle lake. It wanted me to be a boy again, a pre-philatelic type mad for dogs and fishing. The woman herself had disappeared.

I climbed back to my punishment cell in the sky, and from that day never resorted to the window again. My machine had finished with the African translation and was showing an ad for a certain brand of beer in which a satisfied customer was seen lying face-up in a tiny rowboat while drifting at leisure on an ideal lake.

Nineteen

I was on the verge, or "cusp," as moderns like to say, of bringing these considerations to an end when that moment I discerned the wee little philatelic boy waiting on the porch, along with the dog that previously was mine.

"Hail to thee!" I recited. "What the hell you want now, for Christ's sakes?" (I adore naïve people, of which the very last one was living just next door.)

"Want to trade?"

"I always want to trade. What do you have there in that real sloppy collection of yours?"

He opened the album, exposing for the second time just how pitiful it was. The whelp had continued to affix his few dozen stamps with *each stamp's own mucilage*, the first error of amateurs. Even so, I led them inside, where the dog went immediately to his ancient place beneath the gramophone. Next, I took some twenty-five of my own new-style celluloid stamp hinges, an effective product costing about 1.6 cents each, and passed them over to the boy without expecting recompense.

"About two bits' worth," I said. "But I don't ask to be paid."

"Thanks!"

"So! No need even to talk about it, right? It's only a small sum, after all."

"Yes, sir. Say, you don't still have that triangle stamp, do you? The one with the snake on it?"

"Two bits. Just think, Feenie, ten years from now inflation will have turned that into . . . what? A dollar?"

"Yes, sir."

"And when you're rich and fat, Feenie, you can buy as many dogs and hinges as you want. Does that appeal to you?"

"I guess so."

(Having used just three of the hinges, he now tried to return to me the ones left over, the final gesture that confirmed my determination to make him my beneficiary when I be dead.)

"Never give up on it, Feenie, beautiful things, no matter what phase you're in."

He promised.

Twenty

It was on the following day that I carried to work a highly illustrated book with a great many colored plates in it. Recently I have begun trying to identify some of the traits shared by all living thing, for example their presence in space and time and, more strangely still, the desire on the part of even the worst of them to go on living. As for the Polish woman just across the aisle, I wouldn't ask her to see the really extraordinary resemblance she bore to the typical *Anoplogaster cornuta*, a deep-sea creature with a little "lantern" affixed to its snout. An even better comparison is to be seen on page 147, where an unhappy-looking Hairy Frogfish with a tripartite tongue and vestigial eyes appears to be suffering from the unimaginable pressures at that depth. Me, I'd move to higher levels. That was when she (the woman, I mean) turned to me, saying: "Won't be long, Hugh, till you're retired and all! I can just imagine how excited you must be."

I smiled, a successful effort that, like a good old wine, had a bit of the mischievous in it. I sustained it for perhaps six seconds before transitioning over to spoken speech, a less demanding modality.

"Excited? Nothing very exciting about leaving one's friends and colleagues behind. We might never even ever see each other again!"

"Good!" said the bozo in his jocular manner. He was a dear friend of mine, he believed, and had threatened to visit me at some future time. I turned to page 82, settling upon a *Fanfin Seadevil* as his nearest analog. The thing had a goofy smile with all kinds of excrescences everywhere.

I toiled, a fifteen-minute exercise interrupted by a forty-five-minute coffee break in the men's facility on the nineteenth floor. It was my good luck the place was empty—it always was (none but female employees had been assigned to that floor)—and I could read aloud, sometimes even orating in the mirror, an unwise reflex that reflected back to me what I had become.

And then came noon. Getting into my hat and trousers, I would sally out into the free-market realm of money, insincerity, and consensual contempt. (It was of course the sincere ones that presented the greatest danger.) Millions came up to meet me, all of them turning away at the last instant. I passed through a crowd of bored children, blasé before they were ten years old. Within just one block, I encountered no fewer than two hundred liberals, their discontented little faces shuddering with moral indignation. One, the most problematic of them, was wearing stormtrooper boots and had that bony look characteristic of British women. I moved past him without comment. Penis envy was almost extinct now, thanks to the magic of tissue engineering.

That old turpitudinous Leward Pefley, who claimed he could identify the likenesses of Confederate generals in the clouds? No doubt he could, whileas for me it were postage stamps hovering overhead, great ones and small, with a bias toward pre-war East European issues. I halted. Staring at the sky, I believed I could see a farmhouse (turfen roof and yellow pigs) on that one good day in history when love and beauty enveloped everything. Moving out of the traffic (human traffic scattering footprints in the snow), I caught momentary sight in the western sky of the 1930 2 c. yellow Pegasus from Uruguay, a lemon-colored job with a good engraving of my favorite size.

We gathered that night around my kitchen table, me, myself, the two philatelists whom I call "Blue," and "Green," even though their real names were the other way around, and finally the little boy and dog. Unsurprisingly the best collection belonged to an Ashkenazi attorney who had taken control of a nine-album estate that only two days earlier had belonged to a gentile widow lying semi-conscious in a nursing home. He would open these albums and allow us quick glimpses of the riches therein, before then closing them up again and returning to his drink.

"Why don't you let us see the things, for God's sakes?"

"He wants I should let him see my things! Hey! A charity I am? One green American dollar bill—that ain't so much to ask. Hey! And then you can see all you want!"

"You can take it out of the ten dollars you owe me for the drink."

"Oi! I think you're a safety hazard. What is this?"

To say nothing of his face, his fingers were pudgy and short, and so was he. I experienced a desire that some might think wasn't fully consonant with a compassionate human being. Moving quickly, I gathered up the little decorative ashtray that he must pass on his way to the door. In the interval, my friend Blue (I can call him by his right name now) was haggling with the child. We three, we huddled long and appraisingly over a very recherché imperforate of one of the expired colonies of French-speaking France.

It was a pleasant evening spent in the proper way. New York still has one good radio station left over from the 1950s, and by monkeying with the dial, I was able to bring Mahler's Eighth into focus, specifically the much-underrated Abravanel rendition. Of course, I had to dial back and forth frequently to prevent the usual trash music from breaking in upon us from more powerful stations. Yes, and someday there'll be no good music and no good men left anywhere at all.

"Now when you grow up . . ." I started to say.

"Yes, sir, I'm going to study about art and history and stuff."

"And?"

"And if they try to make me join the army, I'll move to another country."

"Excellent! And?"

"I'm going to keep away from all those counterfeit stamps."

"Perfect. You're coming right along. Here, have another drink."

It was full dark by now, and from my place I could see the top stories and svelte steeples of the downtown city. Come the Deluge, the waters will be up to the fortieth stories, I trust, and the indwellers shall either have drowned or dispersed to Africa, Asia, or worse. The only question: Which of those floors higher than forty ought I appropriate for my stamps?

Twenty-One

Here from the fortieth floor of The Empire State Building I stand looking down into the ruined fields of Brooklyn and/or Queens. One lone plowman I see, a sturdy sort of yeoman in a crimson blouse. Methinks I have seen that face before, somewhere in the art of Bruegel. No, it belongs, that face, on bust number nine in the catalog for Easter Island. But it's just an illusion, of course, and great was my dismay when I came back to ground and found myself in the quotidian U.S.A. familiar to us all.

From that elevation I had begun to imagine that the landscape down below was ninety percent Caucasian once again and that little boys were more interested in baseball than in anal intercourse. I enjoyed imagining that people were parts of families, that Hispanics had all been teleported back to Africa, that immigrants were under attack from gene-specific diseases, and as for your garden-variety feminists, that they were being utilized for target practice by our fifty million police. But if I can't have that, let it at least be pleasing to Wotan that the country cease to exist.

Twenty-Two

I have elected to continue with these pages, a project very like retreating off into a dark closet where alone certain truths may be said. Another truth: I had rather been born into the fourteenth century instead of this.

My day of retirement draws nigher! How may I make best use of that long-wished-for moment when I shall toss away my clock, my comb and razor and subway map. I shall vote no more! I will need no longer to participate in smiles and courtesies with two-legged fauna perched behind desks with computers on them. I shall live in the woods with my stamps and the dog that was returned to me on Wednesday. As to that once-promising youth next door, he has gone into another phase and nowadays watches television all day long. I shall amend my will. The stamps I gave him have either been stowed in the attic or thrown out with the garbage, and his mother has kindly asked that I hold no further communication with him.

But meanwhile I continue to report to work, never mind that my fellow commuters have voted me from the group. Today, my bus was late, retarded by some four or five stowaways riding on the roof. Inside, surrounded by somnambulists powered by pills, I again came near to asking the one question most dreaded by our leaders—is this what life is for?

I passed a little old woman, America's waste material, pushing a wheelbarrow holding mops and brooms. Came next a pornographic theater, a suntan salon, a food bank, a video rental, a leather shop, and then a specialty boutique offering Romanian cheeses. I passed a line of parked limousines containing hedge fund operators in need of the guillotine. I bypassed a recumbent tramp spitting up a substance of some sort into the discolored snow. Pushing my mind into the far future, I succeeded in looking upon this as objectively as a Venusian would.

My smiles were wearing ever thinner; even so, I entered my place of work with tremendous cheer, even passing back to Tiffany the magazine I had borrowed all those years ago my first day at work. An ignoramus of the highest water, she loved to see photos of the interiors of the homes of the rich. Some kindly person, the Bozo probably, had left the morning paper on my chair. I gathered it up and commenced to get ready to begin to start my day.

The newspaper: A movie star was getting a divorce. A black child had been offended, and the government was rushing a therapist to the scene. Having refused foreign investment, the bombing of Bolivia had been resumed. Page two revealed that some Americans were continuing to marry inside their own races. Therapists were on their way.

Twenty-Three

It was the evening of that same day that I arrived home to find my abominable son blocking the door. Spawned by my worst wife, he had abandoned us nineteen years ago, carrying nothing but a few CDs of bad music and both my credit cards.

"Hark!" said I, putting on an expansive smile. (I had thought he might be dead by now.) "Well! And so we meet again!"

He grinned, an unsightly business. "Good to have seen you," I said. "Where're you headed?"

"Whoa. I figured I'd crash here for a few days. Like, you know, hey, till I get it all together, right?"

"To be sure. Then you'll probably want to come inside." (Truly, my son is a modern man, which is to say a six-foot hulk of twenty-four-karat shit. On his forearm he has a flawlessly rendered tattoo of an eviscerated woman who must have been beautiful before her mishap. The organs themselves, the kidneys, the spleen, etc., were inscribed on his other arm.)

"I was fired."

"Fired! They must be insane."

"Yeah."

"Where were you working?"

"Aw, this old place in Baltimore. Know what I mean? Dumb sons-of-bitches."

"How ever will they replace you, I wonder?"

"They can't! Shit, I can sell more shit in an hour than those other sons-of-bitches can sell in a day!"

"Not to mention the quality."

"Yeah, right. Say, I was just thinking maybe you'd want to hand over some of my inheritance now, since I'm kind of short these days. My *heritage*—see what I'm saying? I could pay you back later, if that's what you want."

I thought long and deeply over his offer, even taking out a cigarette and plucking thoughtfully at my chin.

"I see what you mean," I reported. "But I've got my heritage all locked up at good interest rates. If I take it out now, you won't get nearly as much later on! I'm not going to leave any money to my other children, you understand."

"Yeah?"

"Absolutely not!"

He smiled. His teeth were worse that I had imagined, one of them comprising nothing more than an adventitious prong with a barb on it.

"How much is it? Naw, I'm just asking. My heritage, I mean."

"Well! Let me just say that you're going to be surprised. *Deeply* surprised."

"Yeah? Hey, 'preciate it, dad. No, really. Can I come

in now?"

He entered anyway, and after stalking through the downstairs rooms, found the refrigerator.

Twenty-Four

He lives there still, on the second story just above my kennel where no amount of threats or discussion makes any impression on his edgy, innovative, and boundary-pushing personality. He snores when I leave home and snores when I come back, saving up the nighttime hours for disappearing into this large and dying city now populated mostly by jigaboos and worse.

The rain that night proved a great consolation, but I slept poorly anyway. Having left the bed three times but urinating only once, I finally got into my Saturday clothes and migrated to the next room with its table, its low-hanging lamp, and philatelic equipment. I could have retired ten years ago, could have I, had only I invested in all those biotechnology start-ups or, heck, just plain simple income-producing utility shares. But then I wouldn't possess these stamps and albums that I see spread out here before me. Suddenly I threw open my Czechoslovak collection and gathered my seventeen-inch magnifying glass.

I could see much, sometimes *too* much, even unto the miniscule messages often left behind by mischievous engravers with nothing better to do. And then, too, I had greatly expanded my knowledge of the boundary conflicts between Hungary and Romania. Not that ever I was able to penetrate the language employed by the former country, a tremendous mess with all sorts of some really screwed-up declensions that lie well outside my rather good knowledge of human tongues and writing systems.

Next I opened on southern South America, and after passing hurriedly over the exiguous postage of Patagonia, arrived at perhaps the most unacknowledged item in that whole volume, a hand-drawn airmail issued more or less as a joke by the members of a weather station positioned on the shelf of Antarctica. Either it was worth a great deal or, some said, had no value at all. It showed a naked woman lap-dancing around the South Pole.

I have seen the art gallery of the Vatican, but my collection, albeit in miniature, is richer than theirs. I keened in upon an Argentine stamp that showed the capitol city and some of the public officials of which the people presumably were proudest. I ought have burnt this stamp right away, except that I needed it to fill the page.

Meantime I had put on the *Tristan* of Melchior, hoping in that way to overcome the noises from upstairs. Congruent with Argentina's so-called "heroic" series, the music formed a backdrop to a set of some dozen stamps picturing some of the noblest figures in Caucasian myth. I bent down close over a medieval boat with colored sails wending its way to Brittany over a vermillion sea.

I viewed insects and waterfalls, portraits of good and evil men, here an escutcheon and there a flower, Spanish buildings, indeed all manner of creatures and products and other matters important to philatelists and normal people alike.

Twenty-Five

My house has been seen by two different realtors, each more cunning than the other. I settled at last on the bald one, who promises me, thanks to the contingencies of zoning laws, an extraordinary price. My current plan is to sell my son along with the building, presuming I can get out of town whilst he lies sleeping. And meantime, day by day, the time of my retirement draws ever nearer.

On Tuesday, I visited the woman next door and insisted on the return of the three stamps I had sold her odious son at bargain rates. This of course led to a rancorous debate in which the woman finally gave expression to the underlying vulgarity, not to mention sheer philistinism, domiciled all these years ago about fifty-three feet from myself, depending upon which part of our two houses we each were occupying at the time.

And then on Tuesday I visited New York's third-best coin, stamp, and antique weapons outlet, where I invested recklessly in a long-time desideratum of mine that I shan't be able to afford unless the house really does fetch the price I've been promised. It hurts me to attend these places, mysterious *endoits* full of superb materials that I, certainly, never shall possess. We grinned at each other, the proprietor and I. His face is long, very long and very narrow, and one of his eyes has been transformed into a "yellow agate," as it were, the aftereffect of an antibiotic allergy.

"You'll want to insure that," he iterated, touching my stamp with the tip of one of his longer fingers.

"Yes, I will," said I. "But I worry about the time I'll need to get to my insurer. I might get robbed."

"Very possible. We have some crazy stamp collectors in this city."

"Philatelists, you mean."

"Of course."

"I stopped being a 'stamp collector' when I was nine years old."

"To be sure. I apologize."

"Some people play golf, while others are *golfers*."

"Don't you just know it. Likewise some people have cars while others have . . ."

"Yes. Strange world out there." He pointed to it.

I paid for the purchase, making use of a traveler's check. The bozo then provided me with an empty tin box that once had held a pricy brand of foreign cigarettes, and after inserting my stamp inside it, accompanied me the first two blocks of my trip to the insurance place. It was a noble building, where that man did business, and bore a Latin inscription above the door that had only the subtlest connection to the activities going on inside. The man with whom I was accustomed to deal was engrossed in tide tables or actuarial tables or something of the kind. I showed him my stamp.

"Nice! What am I supposed to do with it?"

"I need to insure it."

"Ah. Have to get an appraisal, of course. Worth about nineteen cents, would you say?"

"I paid $2,200!"

We looked at each other. Finally he made a remark. His mouth was full of a bright blue tongue and snagged teeth pointing off in all directions. His voice was certainly a New Yorker's.

"$2,200. See this here pencil? Sell it to you for ten thousand. It's got an eraser on it."

I strode hurriedly to work, in my vest pocket a reluctantly-allowed insurance policy granted purely in consideration of our prior arrangements. The sidewalk was crowded, of course, and I relied upon that to hinder burglars and the usual collectors. Arriving at my place, I smiled in turn at everyone, and then slipped the stamp between pages 100 and 101 of the Antonescu memoirs in my top drawer. There remain to me just four days of eight hours each before I am to be turned out into a twenty-first-century world full of stamps and former wives and a third-class airline ticket to ------ in -------.

Twenty-Six

I'm not going to write any more of these memoires; I'm tired and have a great many other things in mind just now. I will say there is to be an auction the day after tomorrow, and I refuse to leave town before having a chance at it. And then, too, I am one of the small number to have been invited to the bidding for the Himmler Collection.

Finally, I will say that I had a dream last night in which my true wife had come back and was bending over me, her eyes sparkling with the love that I had thrown away. It was wrong, I confess it, to have done what I did merely on account of her confusion between the Arabic and Persian scripts. But I was young in those days. Give her back to me—this time I'm begging—give her back and . . .

Ah no, not a chance. I have long ago zipped past the fail-safe point on my path to oblivion and must be satisfied with the joys, if there are any, of a perhaps somewhat elevated form of non-existence among the arts.

GOOD THINGS IN
TINY PLACES[*]

Yesterday, on my way to this meeting place, I stopped at a traffic light and fell suddenly into a burning ring of fire and began to imagine that our purpose here was not merely to discuss the probable future of white people in Western societies, but rather to take real action in an attempt to salvage at least some residue of the Caucasian demographic, Caucasian habits, and the Western high culture. For although we don't judge Caucasians by their present-day behavior, we do know that in the past, unlike most other races, white people *have* sometimes created admirable societies and might do so again. We thought of those cosmologists who search for exoplanets that might be made habitable after our own planet has ceased to exist; likewise, in that same vein, we began to discuss places on Earth that might offer sanctuary for Caucasians who wish to give Western civilization, even if just in miniature scale, another century or two of continued existence.

With that in mind, we voted to send one of our members to sniff out the possibilities in Canada, a large territory to the immediate north of our own country where a fair number of awakened people have already drawn off into the corners of that politically correct domain and have begun to resist the summons of ethnic suicide. That emissary of ours, who

---

[*] On Saturday, March 7, 2015, Tito Perdue read this short story at a banquet in his honor in Atlanta, where he received the first H. P. Lovecraft Prize for Literature.

happens to be here with us today, remained four months, and having at last recuperated from a really very serious case of frostbite, reported back that the Canadians had invested so thoroughly in the theory of universal human equality that no realistic hope remained there for a recrudescence of our traditional culture.

I imagined then that we had assigned yet another agent to the country of Argentina, a South American organization said to have been settled primarily by emigrants from Italy and Spain. A not unpleasant locale, topographically speaking, our representative nevertheless found there a debased and very heterogeneous population only slightly superior to that of Honduras or Haiti, or invertebrate Mexico. At that point we opted to ignore that country, and indeed the entire hemisphere thereto attached.

We tried Australia, but not for very long. From having once enjoyed the best immigration policy in the world, that island has recently discovered a need for ever larger numbers of hard-working but unsmiling Chinese. With a white fertility ratio now in negative territory, the Australians are looking even further afield for new citizens, including especially in such locales as American Indian reservations, Lapland, Detroit, Kirgizstan, and the Central African Republic. On the bright side, they *have* abrogated some of the rules and regulations directed against English speakers.

In the wake of these disappointments, we met again eighteen months later in an inconspicuous town (not named here) in southwest Nebraska, a place rarely visited by the national media. It *is* true that a bitter debate broke out on the second day, and that our former fellowship was damaged by a much-too-vehement debate in which four of the members spoke for remaining in America and continuing the struggle *here at home* for the resumption of racial inequality. The motion was voted down, however, whereupon one of the attendees got suddenly to his feet, made a hissing noise, departed, and never came back again.

It wasn't until the third week of our conference that the delegate from New York, a certain Chris Martin, mentioned the name of a place called New Zealand as a possibility. His suggestion was at first received with silence. Known mostly for America's remoteness from that place, and its strange fauna, we needed time to absorb the suggestion. Comprised mostly of two large islands with a gap between them, the country was known to have been settled in 1840 by British people who without great effort were able to impose themselves on the aboriginal people, who quickly learned to get the hell out of the way. Dismayed by the quality of the natives, the fair-minded British nevertheless refrained from what they could so easily have done, even allowing those people to marry and own property, and to sustain themselves as a certain percentage of the population.

Despite that, the culture of those islands was said to be distinctly European, more European indeed than most parts of modern Europe itself. As for the topography, the lakes and rivers, woods and fields, the mountains and their requisite valleys, these features have come together just about perfectly in this most inviting of all locations. Especially the South Island is regarded by connoisseurs as among the most gorgeous acreages in the whole wide world. Our delegate needed very little time to verify this description and then come running back to us with his eyes all aglow.

And so as I continued dreaming, I imagined that by October five of us, together with our families, had made the long journey by sea to New Zealand's South Island, where we wasted the first several days accustoming ourselves to the southern sky, with its odd-looking constellations. But this was nothing as compared to the upside-down seasons, which became more and more abnormal the further south we traveled. It was late September by this time, a propitious season more or less equal in quality to early April in more northerly parts. Never will I forget it, the supernal views that offered themselves as we squeezed our way through the channel that divides the two main islands. I thought I saw a flight of kiwi birds overhead, which is to say until I was informed that those creatures had long ago lost their penchant for flying.

We wasted two further weeks behaving like tourists, but by October we had found homes for ourselves in a picturesque village in the island's south-easternmost quadrant. The views were excellent, and the water not as frigid as has all too unthinkingly been imputed to the Pacific Ocean. The schools were good, too, most of them, and the citizenry spoke a better grade of English than did us interlopers. The price of real estate wasn't greatly unlike what prevailed in the United States, and for the most part the national diet was not altogether unacceptable. As you can see, we were already thinking of applying for citizenship, and except for the presence of some 22,000 Maori aborigines, would probably have done so before the first two months were out. You must remember, too, that we were retired people with sufficient income or, in the case of the Albercrombie family, wealthy enough to offer non-assumable five- and ten-year loans at a rate only slightly more than twice that of prevailing Treasury Notes. Opportunities for employment were limited, it is true, and yet we had no hesitation in summoning our friends and relatives to come and join us.

At this point I will admit that it needed some courage to denounce our American citizenship and to become authentic New Zealanders with all the responsibilities and benefits thereunto attached. We had to adjust to a new social code that allowed us to speak to neighbors, or even strangers, without being chided for our genetic identity. Slowly and slowly, we became aware that our island was not dropping bombs *on any other country*, no matter how weak and small. And I can honestly testify that I have seen twelve- and thirteen-year-old boys and girls enjoying each other's company *even in the absence of full penetration.*

Friends and relatives—they came slowly at first, reluctant to leave behind a country that had produced the Antebellum South and had once given promise of developing into something like ancient Greece, or Florence, or London in Elizabeth's day. Instead of that, the United States had merely gotten rich and powerful, and more and more detestable with each succeeding election. Particularly it was the election of 2024 that drove more than four hundred American Caucasian families to our little island and made possible the election of some of our own people to local offices. Truth is, we had already become an identifiable demographic despised by some and applauded by others. Evidence of hostility had quickly broken out in the township of Riverton, a widely reported event that revealed what sort of people were these American newcomers who not only spoke with an accent, but also had refused to surrender their guns at the border. Month by month, the island's young people came to us, demanding to be given a role in the rioting and the electioneering that followed in our wake.

We were bolstered by the people of Invercargill, a largish town of some fifty thousand souls, the first to rally to our cause. Came next Dunedin, where the town council agreed to hear us out. By this time we numbered better than two thousand, and had won the support, or anyway the tolerance of an appreciable minority of the island's voters. Polls showed that no less than thirty-one percent of the people were glad for our presence on the island, or at least were not overtly hostile to our project of prolonging Western civilization for another century or more.

We were a Faustian race, we tried to explain, who had come to fulfill and then to supersede itself. Thus we recommended ourselves, boasting that we were of the same race as had given more to life than all the others added up together. Our own country, we explained, had surrendered to the imperial temptation and had by now become so heterogeneous that a coherent culture was no longer feasible. Life in America, we went on, now required a degree of cultural toleration indistinguishable from nihilism.

But what we mostly understood was that the notion of across-the-board universal wall-to-wall categorical human equality was, as Alex Kurtagić has shown, the most immoral and most suicidal concept ever to find acceptance in an educated, or anyway a semi-educated, nation. He saw, did Alex, that equality and quality hate each other, and that an equal society is perforce a lowest-common-denominator society that will always be finding new ways to slough off standards and to marginalize its own best people. And finally we understood that an equal society will soon become unequal again, except that this time it will be the worst who are considered the best, and the best the worst.

We understood, too, that in post-modern times television has the authority to nudge people in any direction the producers want, while at the same undermining even the most instinctual and time-honored traditions. We understood, too, that we had in our midst a man so very rich that he could take control, if he so wished, of the island's most important television network.

By this time, our numbers had increased to just more than eight-and-a-half thousand, good persons, most of them, and venturesome enough to bring their savings, their relatives, and their experience in starting businesses and commercial operations. Some were merely opportunists of course, ordinary folk fleeing conditions in the U.S. and in Europe, where the demographics were turning more and more decidedly against white people and their standards. Which is not to say that those standards weren't also in a state of advanced decay. Indeed, it had become difficult to say whether it were the immigrants who were degrading the United States, or the United States that was degrading the immigrants. Because decadence, feeding on the applause of the masses, had become irreversible by now.

Timaru, a maritime city that overlooks the sea, was the first place in New Zealand to fall under our sway. Having elected a majority of the town council, we summoned together the some 158 Maori aborigines who lived in the vicinity and offered each man and women of them a full 1,500 New Zealand dollars to emigrate and not come back again. Those willing to undergo sterilization were offered twice that amount, a promise that nearly bankrupted the city treasury. It is hard to describe the anger directed at us by the island's good-thinking people, not to mention the reaction in the international press. The United Nations had involved itself, and we were summoned to appear before the International Court. On the other hand, the town's expatriate population more than doubled in the following seven months with people from nearby towns beginning to cluster around the three villages we now controlled. We were in some danger of comprising a *city*, until the authorities, just in the nick of time, made that impossible.

The rest of the story is well-known to you, how by 2028, we had managed to gain a permanent electoral majority over the entire island and could begin at last to put into effect the policies that had inspired us from the start. Determined to evade the banality of democracy, we wanted to accomplish that which never before had ever been tried, namely to put in place a governing elite composed of people who were able to *think,* recognizing as we did that the overwhelming majority of human beings are capable merely of taking into account half a dozen prevailing orthodoxies and then choosing the one or two that promise to be the least demanding. For our part, we wanted to build a community prepared to give no better than ten percent of its energies to economics and the remaining part to matters of importance, the exact reverse of established practice up until that point. In short, we wanted to break through the glass ceiling of human nature and begin the process of obsolescing ourselves. We wanted to organize our own evolution and become a new species.

Of course it was dangerous. Of course there were China and the United States to contend with. The United Nations, NATO, the EU, bilateral trade agreements, the Kansas City Flower Club—all these organizations and institutions would want to put us out of business as promptly as possible and sink our little island beneath the waves. And who could blame them? If our experiment were successful, it would prove the whole world had been hideously mistaken over the most recent five thousand years.

In the event, it happened that we had a certain famous toxicologist in our town, a man as devoted to our adventure as anyone well could be. He it was who gave us the safety we desired. Too small and too poor to develop nuclear weapons, far less the needed delivery systems, our man "cooked up," so to speak, two tons of a certain highly contagious virus that must not be mentioned here by actual name. Thereafter it was an easy matter for our agents to stow vacuum-sealed containers of this material in the major cities of the several countries that might pose a threat.

For our further defense, we listened to the island's foremost Classical scholar, who described for us how some of the veterans of Alexander had formed themselves into an army called "The Silver Shields," a force of septuagenarians who were to prove the most terrifying fighting force of the age. Widowers, most of them, whose children had grown up and become independent, these were people who had little to live for, and who cared not at all for their own survival. With effort, we were able to identify some 1,626 such people from among our own population, 70 and 75 and yes, even some 80-year-olds trained to bench press their own weight and run five miles in under an hour. Posted at intervals along our shores, they defended us most adequately from tourists, immigrants, refugees, and photo-journalists from the *New York Times*. Even better, they defeated all attempts by the North Island, now only ninety-two percent white, to force us to reunite.

I should add that in 2023 there really was an attempted landing on our island by a force of North Islanders trained and supplied by the U.S. Department of Education in conjunction with the American-Israel Public Affairs Committee. This attempted invasion failed utterly, owing to the courage and skill of some few dozen elderly "hoplites," we call them, four of whom sacrificed themselves in the effort. Since that time, no other attempt has been made against our fortress home.

And all this time the Committee had been steadily at work on our new constitution, or as we call it, our Confession of Sovereign Laws. We had wanted an organic document that would militate unambiguously *against* consumerism as a lifestyle, *against* feminism, *against* globalism and universal rights, but *for* a high culture making constant war against the ever-present aggressions of the low culture that yearns for tawdriness in all walks of life. Most of all we were adamant against immigration and the racial deterioration consequent thereunto. We wanted a society that preferred quality to equality; indeed, we sought a final termination of the very name and notion of equality, believing as we did that not even sub-atomic particles could be found to be equal in all respects, far less automobiles, or horses, or restaurants, or cultures, or works of music and literature. Equality, we hold, is simply a capitulation to mediocrity and, finally, sub-mediocrity all the way down to the current practice of the decaying U.S.A.

We wanted our philosophy to suffuse the island under the leadership of our best, or anyway our least benighted, citizens. In pursuance of that, we needed penalties that were neither too severe nor yet too lax. In short, we wanted penalties that were just right. For

minor crimes—such as littering, loud music, the mis-
treatment of dogs, loose trousers, and pigtails—we
assigned a period of hard labor in reforestation pro-
jects, highway clean-up, and the like. For crimes of
the middling sort, permanent expulsion was the punishment and the only one. But for the most egregious
forms of behavior—treason, rape, book theft, and
child molestation—the punishment cannot be described where sensitive people may be present. Save
to report that it *is* related to one of the creatures held
for that purpose in the national aquarium.

We called our organization *The Node*, named after
a certain piece of classical American fiction. Our
group was to be very, very hard to enter, and easy,
very easy to be expelled from. With an income stipu-
lated to be no higher than the island's average, we
removed greed from any possible motive of ours.
Nepotism was strictly disallowed, and since decisions
were not attributed to individuals, we hoped also to
remove the desire for prestige from our members' mo-
tives. We wanted, in short, to behave like experi-
mental philosophers questing for a form of civilization that might prove significantly less awful than any
that had gone before.

But is with our national budget that we have most
clearly given expression to our intentions. With a
population of white people, welfare benefits were seldom needed, and because we had no role in international connections, we had only to pay for a certain
tonnage of viral material, together with shotgun shells
for our army of old men. Taken all together, our defense budget consumed just 3.2 percent of revenue, a
tiny sum compared to the 12.8 percent dedicated to
the national library, 9.9 percent for one major and
three regional Wagnerian opera houses, 7.4 percent

for six publishing firms that were freed by this allocation from having to show a profit, 9.6 percent for a new radio telescope to be set up on Mount Tasman, and 5.1 percent for the new National Gallery of Unpretentious Art. Apart from another 15.5 percent for other basic and required expenses, we were left with 7.4 percent for the education of generic people and 29.1 percent for the gifted, which is to say approximately 2 percent of the island's population. More than any other country, we specialized in the development of intellectual excellence and the promotion of genius. Five years of this and the island led all international rankings of educational success on a per-capita basis. And though we have but four universities, they have easily supplied us with the sort of men who in course of time will be invited to join the Committee.

And so this is it, ladies and gentlemen, this is what passed through my mind as I waited for the traffic light to change from red to green.

ABOUT THE AUTHOR

Tito Perdue was born in 1938 in Chile, the son of an electrical engineer from Alabama. The family returned to Alabama in 1941, where Tito graduated from the Indian Springs School, a private academy near Birmingham, in 1956. He then attended Antioch College in Ohio for a year, before being expelled for cohabitating with a female student, Judy Clark. In 1957, they were married, and remain so today. He graduated from the University of Texas in 1961, and spent some time working in New York City, an experience which garnered him his life-long hatred of urban life. After holding positions at various university libraries, Tito has devoted himself full-time to writing since 1983.

His first novel, 1991's *Lee*, received favorable reviews in *The New York Times, The Los Angeles Reader*, and *The New England Review of Books*. Since then, he has published sixteen other novels—including *The New Austerities* (1994), *Opportunities in Alabama Agriculture* (1994), *The Sweet-Scented Manuscript* (2004), *Fields of Asphodel* (2007), *The Node* (2011), *Morning Crafts* (2013), *Reuben* (2014), the *William's House* quartet (2016), *Cynosura* (2017), *Philip* (2017), *The Bent Pyramid* (2018), and *Though We Be Dead, Yet Our Day Will Come* (2018)—which have been praised in *Chronicles: A Magazine of American Culture, The Quarterly Review, The Occidental Observer*, and at *Counter-Currents*.

In 2015, he received the H. P. Lovecraft Prize for Literature.